Dakar Diary

586-MCNE

Dakar Diary

My 1960-62 Experiences
While Serving at
U.S. Embassy, Senegal

To: Verna and Bill
With fond memories of our
voyage across the Atlantic and
sunny days in Portugal.
FROM: Elizabeth McNeill-Leicester
Fort Lauderdale
20 May 2007

Elizabeth
McNeill-Leicester

Library of Congress Number: 2002090602
ISBN :   Softcover   1-4010-4850-1

This book was printed in the United States of America.

To order additional copies of this book, contact:
Xlibris Corporation
1-888-795-4274
www.Xlibris.com
Orders@Xlibris.com

Contents

DEDICATION

TO MY SISTER, DORIS ANNE WALL,
A FAITHFUL CORRESPONDENT DURING MY STAY
IN DAKAR.

ALSO BY THE AUTHOR

TAIRONIAN GOLD—Xlibris

PROLOGUE

Dakar Diary, from 23 August 1960 to 12 March 1962, was compiled from letters I wrote while posted to the American Embassy, Dakar, Senegal, French West Africa. Under cover of an assistant Consular Officer I worked for the Central Intelligence Agency (CIA) and, therefore, have divulged no details of my duties. In most cases I have used true first names of people who appear in this diary.

PART I

DAKAR 1960

(Tuesday 23 August)

Sun glinting through shutters brought me out of a deep sleep of exhaustion. Still in my panties and bra and bathed in perspiration, I felt paralyzed to move from the bed. As I looked around the shabby, sweltering, unfamiliar room the musty odor of the tropics brought me back to reality.

A few hours ago, at 4:35 a.m., I arrived at my diplomatic post in Dakar, Senegal, French West Africa (delayed in Paris because of a bloodless *coup d'etat* in Senegal). I stepped off the plane into the humid African night, smelling of rotting vegetation. The sleepy customs officer, in his wilted blue uniform, came to attention, took my passport, paged through it, eyed me with disdain and handed it back with a comment I didn't understand. I sensed that something was wrong. I asked him, in my halting French, to speak slowly.

By the time he had repeated his still unintelligible remark, a handsome man with short, thick, black hair, olive skin and black bushy eyebrows, rushed to my rescue. It was my new boss Frank, speaking Parisian French with appropriate hand gestures.

"What do you mean," he said to the official, "she doesn't have a proper visa?" He turned to me. "Unbelievable!" He threw up his arms in despair. "Your Mali Federation visa is stamped 'Transit Without Stopping' and yet," he shook his head in disbelief, "it clearly states that you are assigned to the American Embassy at Dakar. How stupid," he muttered under his breath.

After a heated back and forth between my boss and the customs official he reluctantly released me into Senegal without a recognized government to give me a visa to remain. Senegal had broken the Mali Federation and hadn't been recognized yet by the U.S.A.

In my groggy state, the long ride along the coastal road to the city had seemed endless. We talked about Paris and my flight from the States. When we reached the dark, silent city my boss pointed out the Embassy on the way to the hotel. He apologized for putting me in such a shabby hotel, "But," he added, "it's close to the office."

The black, shiny-faced bellhop deposited my bags in a small room with a private shower, but no toilet. The nearest one was a Turkish type (hole in the floor over which one squats). When the door closed behind the bellhop I started to undress, but obviously got only as far as my underwear before collapsing into a deep sleep.

This morning after a continental breakfast, served on a tray on my balcony, I found the office, a five-story building, only a few blocks away on the corner of a large open square. When I saw the stars and stripes, waving from a flag pole outside the second floor, I thought the whole building was the Embassy. What a disappointment! The Embassy occupied only the second floor. The entire staff were crowded into small rooms of what was meant to be a large apartment. An automobile showroom and the French Maritimes booking agent took up the ground floor.

I arrived at 0830. The French receptionist already knew my name and greeted me with a smile and "Bon jour!" as though I was anxious to jump right into French. She escorted me to my new office in the Consular Section. My predecessor, in her late twenties, was a bouncy, cloak-and-dagger type who regarded her work as "fun and games." She seemed eager to see what the new "body" looked like. I gathered that both she and the boss were pleased. A look at my boss in the daylight revealed nice soft-brown eyes. I had heard that he was first generation French/American. He's extremely polite and has a coating of 'old world charm'.

Facing me in the office were two great hazards: on my desk perched a large, hulking, electric typewriter, which I didn't know how to use. We still used manuals in India. Above my desk whirred a wobbly fan, of which we had plenty in India and I hated them. There was no air-conditioning and fans had to be kept going at full blast.

(Monday 29 August)

My boss and his wife, a blond all-American Smith College grad, my predecessor and other Embassy staff members wined and dined me all last week, but now I must face eating alone in restaurants. The food is not very good and terribly expensive: $3.00 for dinner! But I've been told we get a good "cost of living" allowance, so I can afford it.

Today I looked at a small villa apartment, turned down by the last woman to arrive at the Embassy. I liked it and will probably live there. First it has to be renovated. It has possibilities. Apartments are almost impossible to find.

(Wednesday 31 August)

Having seen pictures of the handsome Senegalese in their long flowing robes, called *boubous*, I expected to see them gracefully maneuvering the hazardous potholed streets. Instead most of the people in the streets were unattractive white people, French *colons* primarily. Men in very short shorts and women in shorts and halters or homemade cotton dresses. The older women with toasted-brown wrinkled skin looked rather hard. Results of too much sun? The French military still have installations here and a few French officials remain in the government. Other nationalities include diplomats and oil company employees on holiday. Most of the foreign Embassy employees live near here in the Presidential palace area.

(Friday 2 September)

At my last post in New Delhi I was in the political section, completely off limits to unauthorized persons. Marines guarded the Embassy's main entrance. We could lock our office doors. But here in Dakar I'm in the Consular Section, wide open to the public. My boss and I are both under Consular cover. He is the Consul Officer, but his Embassy consular assistant does most of the work while he attends to CIA business.

My boss is very social and all ready I can see that I'll be forced to spend my days being social with my boss' many French and Senegalese friends, who drop in to see about visa applications, or just to read our copy of the *Paris Herald Tribune*. As a result, I will have to do my secret work at night. In addition to these conditions, I have to battle a fan that blows secret documents out onto the open balcony behind my desk. I have to keep the French doors open otherwise I would suffocate.

My big IBM electric typewriter still intimidates me and adds to my frustration. Using it makes me tense, I tend to leave my fingers resting on the keys, thus producing unwanted letters, which means a lot of time-consuming retyping. To defeat the fan, which wrecked my Paris hairdo, I had my hair cut, but conquering the IBM beast will not be as easy. In addition to waking up in the middle of the night wondering if I'd locked all the safes, I now have to ask: Did I turn off my typewriter?

(Saturday 3 September)

Yesterday my trunk arrived, by air freight, to further crowd me in my tiny hotel room. But I will now have more cotton dresses to tide me over until I can find a solution to the laundry problem.

Last night my predecessor's farewell party, attended by some of her French boy friends, introduced me to Dakar nightlife. After a sumptuous dinner at the boss' house, he and his wife took us to a new African night club, on the water. The French love to dance, especially the cha-cha-cha. We stayed until 0400. None of the Frenchmen were my type. Alas! All the "nice" people are in France to escape the heat, I've been told.

This morning I felt ill and depressed so I stayed in bed and read Francoise Sagan' latest play, *Chateau en Suede.*

I bought (ostensibly, since it belongs to CIA) my predecessor's small French car (*Renault deux chaveaux*) and plan to travel all I can in this small country.

(Sunday 4 September)

I'm sitting on the balcony outside my fourth floor hotel room. It is one of those beautiful after-the-rain early mornings. A cool, crisp sea breeze gently brushes my warm cheeks. I can smell something (lamb) being roasted over an open charcoal fire. I can see, towering above red-tiled roofs and lush green trees, a scattering of buildings, dazzling-white against a periwinkle-blue sky. The Cathedral bells call the devout to worship. African children playing in the streets below my balcony are making happy sounds in their own strange language, *wolof*. As I sit here, suspended above it all, I'm thinking of my Sundays in other countries and wondering, as I did then, if someday I will have someone with whom to share this special day.

Sunday has always been special. As a child I used to daydream of faraway places during those early-morning, silent hours, when my parents and siblings were still asleep. It was always a peaceful day, a family day. Since then there have been hundreds of Sundays in faraway places, but I no longer daydream. And I am no longer as lonely as I was the first few years on my own. Be it Sunday or Monday, I now feel that it is **my** day and with it I have the possibility of creating something beautiful.

Yet, this morning I feel disenchanted. It is hard to sort out the various factors contributing to this state of mind. But I must make an effort. Realism at this point is very important. If I'm to continue being independent I have to work. And since I have chosen this career, which allows me to live in exotic countries, then I must stop whining and get on with it. Disinterest in my surroundings probably stems from the fact that I don't want to believe that I will be spending the next two years here. After India, which I loved, Dakar is a letdown. And after six months of freedom in Paris I resent having to return to this way of life. Usually when I go to a new country I imagine all sorts of exciting moments awaiting me around every corner and through every mile of the countryside. But here, I refuse to look beyond my immediate surroundings. Perhaps because I have no hope of finding happiness here. Surely, it can't be that at thirty seven I'm already one of those lonely, frustrated career women in whose faces are written a thousand sad stories. Have I become so self-sufficient that no one thinks of my feelings, or need for help. If I should break down under the strain, I would probably be dismissed as a peculiar, neurotic, frustrated old maid and life would go on without a word of sympathy or understanding from anyone. So I must be strong and confide my true feelings only in my diary. But I must never write about my work, which makes it difficult to explain why I'm frustrated and exhausted from having to work at night.

(Monday 5 September)

I left my hotel this morning about 8:45 and for a moment I couldn't understand why the streets were so crowded. Election day! Of course. Now that the Mali Federation no longer exists Senegal must elect a President. At the sight of all the colorful costumes my conscience pricked me. The 16mm movie camera and color films my brother gave me before I left for Dakar had not been used. These were the very scenes he wanted me to capture.

When I reached the Square I met an Embassy officer standing on the curb holding his movie camera. That settled it! I ran back to my hotel room and scooped up my camera. For one hour we waited. The crowd of onlookers, neither dense nor enthusiastic, already knew the results. It was only a formality. The president is chosen by the Parliament.

We were about to give up when the shiny-black faces of the mounted, red-coated, presidential guards appeared around the corner. I got so excited that the Embassy officer had to jerk me away from the horses hooves.

When all the red coats and waving dignitaries, in open cars, disappeared from my tiny camera lens I had done my duty and now could enjoy the parade. But it was over. I was furious. This is the very thing I dislike about taking photos. One never gets to see anything. Now I will have to wait until the film is developed to see the parade. If the film doesn't turn out, I missed the parade.

(Wednesday 7 September)

Last night I had a real fright. About midnight I was burning secret trash in a potbellied stove on the second-floor open balcony. I have to burn trash at night after the Embassy is closed, because I'm not supposed to have secret trash. Following my predecessor's instructions I shredded the secret documents into a trash bag, built a fire in the potbellied stove on the balcony and then, with the lid off, I fed the fire with the shredded documents. I was sleepily watching the flames shoot out the top of the stove when apparently the upstairs neighbor smelled the smoke. Her head appeared over the balcony and her wide eyes stared down at the flames. She started screaming FEU! FEU! I slammed the lid on the stove and tried to explain, in my poor French, that I was only burning papers. I begged her not to call the fire department. Through my mind raced an image of firemen bursting through the Embassy doors, their high-powered hose sweeping everything before them, drenching me, turning the potbellied stove into a sizzling ball of steam, while all the occupants of the apartments above leaned over the balcony, watching. But, thank goodness, the woman stopped screaming. I grabbed the secret trash bag and fled into my office and locked the French doors. I worried all night, after I went to bed, about not stirring those secret ashes three times to be sure not one scrap of paper survived.

(Thursday 8 September)

Went to the beach with my boss and his wife and three children. It was the first time I'd been outside my little circle between the hotel and the Embassy. The countryside, especially now during the rainy season, is sprinkled with green vegetation. African villages of round thatched huts, protected by a flimsy palisade of sticks, dotted the landscape.

Senegal has more than 350 miles of beaches and many surround Dakar, but we drove about thirty minutes to one with miles of bone-white sand, warm water and few people. It was perfect. Not a vendor in sight. Young African boys frolicked on the beach stark naked. European women of all sizes, shapes and ages wore tiny bikinis. I felt overdressed in my conservative two-piece American bathing suit. When I get my license I will drive out there alone and walk for miles along the sea.

My correspondence with Ernst has flared up again for the second time since we parted in Paris over seven months ago. He thinks it's very important that we see one another. He planned to stop in Dakar, on his way from Argentine to Paris, this month, but now it looks as though he will have to fly straight through. He still wants to meet me somewhere. Maybe the Canary Islands. Since no one else has replaced him in my life, I do miss him; and sometimes it's a great comfort to know that he still cares for me. He's into some business deal and hopes it will bring him a steady income so he can settle down. With me? I have little hopes. An artist from an aristocratic Swedish family he is inexperienced in a stable, financial way of life. We shall see. Thinking of him makes me homesick for India. We were happy together there. He was the perfect companion for roaming about that vast continent from the Himalayas to Ceylon.

Politically everything here is quiet. The Mali/Senegal Federation is finished, but the Republic of Senegal has not been recognized by any foreign country. I think it is only a matter of time until both Senegal and Mali are recognized as separate countries. No trouble is envisaged.

My negative and unreasonable attitude towards having to continue working takes such stupid forms. Some times I find myself disliking the people I pass in the streets, especially unattractive French people, as though it were their fault that I am here.

I'm tired of "starting over again." So rather than rushing out to see the wonders of Senegal, I just lie on the bed in my cramped hotel room and read as though it will all go away if I take no notice. I'm sure this, too, will pass and lots of pleasant moments await me in the next two years.

I hate eating out alone in the evening. I have lost five pounds, down to 115. Too thin for my five foot seven height. Tomorrow I get my driver's license. I can try out my little *deux chevaux* and be independent again.

(Friday 9 September)

Some local prices: Postage to the States for one sheet of paper costs about .22 cents. From the states it's only .10 cents. For lunch I used to spend $3.00, but now I've found a little place near one of the markets, where I can get the menu of the day, which is usually good, plus wine for less than $2.00. A cake of ordinary bath-size soap, .75 cents, .15 cents in the States. Whiskey, cigarettes and some food stuffs come in duty free. I will make out all right and hope to save enough to break free of this solitary life.

It takes weeks to get anything done. I had hoped to receive my driver's license today. I have already given 1,700 francs ($1.00 buys 245 Senegalese francs) and four photos. But, alas, it will take another week. I wanted to set off on my own this weekend. I think I'll "chance" it anyway and drive to one of the beaches on Saturday. I am reading *The Rage Of Vultures*, by Alan Moorehead.

I hope the work on my villa-apartment is finished by October. Yet this enjoyable period, of having no household responsibilities, makes adjusting to life here a bit easier. I've arranged with a French bachelor, who will return to France at the end of November, to take over his servant. From what I have heard, he can do everything, including the laundry. He is worth waiting for. My household effects from India will probably arrive in early December.

Attending several French-speaking parties has improved my French.

(Saturday 10 September)

I have just returned from the beach and am drinking a coca cola. In the back of my mind I'm trying to conjure the French for "Sorry, I have an engagement this evening." My boss told me that a Frenchman I met the other night is going to call me to go dancing this evening, but I have no desire to see him. He seems second-class and dull.

(Sunday 11 September)

My first full day at the beach and I'm red as a lobster almost all over, after modifying my bathing suit. Even so I felt overdressed. The women here wear the briefest two bands of cloth possible.

I set out this morning feeling adventurous and a bit scared, driving all alone without a license. I had a bit of trouble getting on the coastal road, known as the corniche, but once I got started it was exciting. A great feeling of freedom exhilarated me. I was off on an adventure all my own.

I didn't see another car for miles on the corniche road, snaking up and along the cliffs, overlooking the blue Atlantic. When the road came near the edge of the cliff my fear of heights kept me from looking down at the ocean, far below. Beautiful homes, surrounded by lush, tropical landscaping along the road gave me an entirely new view of Dakar.

After about thirty minutes I arrived at the popular beach, stretching out between the modern N'Gor hotel and the lagoon-like Atlantic. Masses of people, mostly white, swarmed over the 'talcum-powder' sand dotted with umbrellas and mattresses for hire. Small cabins and a snack bar, serving wine and delicious French food, lined the space between the beach and the hotel. The blue Atlantic, like an enormous saltwater swimming pool, stretched out to a small island. I enjoyed being alone, swimming, lying on a comfortable mattress under an umbrella, reading and dozing after a delicious *salade Niçoise* and a glass of cold, white wine.

(Wednesday 14 September)

The work on my villa apartment is slow. The kitchen and bathroom are being completely redone. There are no closets, so I'm having one made in an alcove in the living room. This is an old colonial house, probably built in the early twenties. The electrical wiring, installed after the house was built, is now unsafe and has to be replaced. At the moment the rooms are painted in shocking pink and bright blue with a mustard yellow trim. I'm thinking of pale gray walls with white trim.

(Friday 16 September)

The British Ambassador's wife, an American I met in Washington, D. C., had a cookout for the British and American

Embassy staffs. Among the single women was my opposite number in the British Embassy, Pat, an attractive woman of medium height, short wavy dark hair and darting blue eyes, which gave her the appearance of being self-conscious. A bit younger than I am, she was a friend of my predecessor. I was shocked when she talked about her secret work. Apparently she and my predecessor talked openly to one another about their job. I'm sure they got along well, being the young, dramatic cloak and dagger types.

(Tuesday 20 September)

Across the street, below my fourth-floor balcony, the French flag has just been raised on the Army barracks, signifying, I suppose, that the sun is up, but it is not in evidence. Gray-blue clouds cover the sky, but the rainy season has supposedly ended until next July. What an awful thought, now all the lush green will turn brown. I have noticed already that the breeze is less and less. October is said to be the worst because there is neither breeze, nor rain. I'm surprised that I have not suffered unduly from heat and humidity, but I must admit I could work better if the office were air conditioned. I'm looking forward to winter months, by that time I should be in my apartment..and might even have my driver's license and will be a legal driver.

The U.S. still hasn't recognized Senegal. At the moment we are here as guests, so we dare not move about very much.

(Wednesday 21 September)

I had dinner with British Pat. She studied in Paris and speaks French fluently with a beautiful accent. Makes me feel inadequate. She hates Dakar, but luckily has to stay only eighteen months. We have to serve twenty-four. The difference in living allowance between us and the Brits is most notable in the way we each live. I have a large villa flat. Hers is small and sparsely furnished. I have a "company" car. She doesn't. But these things don't seem to matter to her. She is used to not having all the perks that her opposite number in the American Embassy has. They think we are spoiled. And we are. But she doesn't work half as hard as I do and their policy of serving only eighteen months in a 'hardship' post is more humane. The Brits are more sensible about the importance of the 'communist' threat to Senegal, even though their colony, British Gambia, borders Senegal. While, as far as I can see, we have no U.S.A. interests in Senegal. It's France's responsibility. Yet we work like maniacs combating "communism". Dakar doesn't have much of a communist party, if any.

(Saturday 24 September)

Took Patricia, new girl in the Embassy to the beach. She's young, attractive, tall with sparkling dark eyes, full of enthusiasm and a good companion. This is her first post and I wonder if she can tough it out. The State Department should never send pretty, young women to Dakar for their first post, especially if they don't speak French. They lack the resources to survive without male companionship and there's not one acceptable eligible bachelor in our Embassy.

We came home early because we each had a dinner engagement. I went to dinner with the Assistant Cultural Affairs Officer, Jolée, a young, very attractive and charming black woman from the States. It was one of the nicest evenings I have spent here, because I met some Africans; two high-ranking government officials, one is married to a French woman as are many high-ranking government officials, including the Senegalese President. The few Senegalese women present were dressed in the latest Paris fashions. Pity, without their flowing boubous and frothy turbans they looked quite ordinary.

Jolée speaks beautiful French. A whole evening in Senegalese French exhausted me. I hoped we'd be good friends because she is the only American I have met who is really interested in African art and culture as I am. Through her I hoped to see some of the countryside and be accepted into African society. But, alas, before the evening was over she announced that she would be leaving soon.

(Sunday 25 September)

I was up early for horseback riding. British Pat couldn't go, but the Charge d'affaires' 14-year-old daughter, Alice, went with me. We'd booked horses at the Riding Club, but they had been taken by someone else, so we spent a great part of the morning driving all over Dakar looking for horses to ride. We finally found some out near the beach and had a wonderful ride through a fishing village (a few huts shaded by acacia trees) and then along the beach. My horse stumbled and I fell off, but landed on my feet and jumped right back on again. We finished riding about eleven and by noon I was at the beach with American Pat and Carmen, another single woman in our Embassy.

The three of us took out a big surf board with paddles. After playing around in the middle of the bay, diving off the board or just lying face down, looking at the fish in the clear, deep water. When we'd had too much sun we headed back toward the beach on the big surf board. Pat in front, Carmen in the middle and I was on the back. Pat and I decided to stand up and paddle, a difficult balancing act. We were going along very well when Carmen suddenly stood up and started the board rocking. I tried to keep my balance because I didn't want to fall in and lose my prescription sun glasses, but before I realized it Pat and Carmen tumbled in, letting the board fly up just as I lost my balance and fell forward. The board hit the right side of my face before I fell into the water. For a moment I was sure my right jaw was broken. The pain was so strong I couldn't speak. I thought I was going to pass out in the water, but finally I surfaced and cried for help. They got me back onto the board and floated me to the beach.

(Monday 26 September)

The teeth in my right jaw are still numb and last night when I was washing my hair my nose spurted blood. I had a hard time getting it stopped. I just hope everything is all right. I dread to think what medical care is like here.

I have been here one month and three days. It's strange I can hardly remember the first day here. But my two bonus days in Paris still glow in my memory. I was sitting at a sidewalk cafe on the Champs-Elysées when I heard about the *coup d'état* in Senegal. I hurriedly paid the check and rushed back to the Embassy, where I was told to remain in Paris until the situation cleared in Dakar. I remember those days vividly. I had extra time with friends to roam about, have coffee at the *Deux Maggot* once more and see Ionesco's play, *"La Cantatrice Chauve"*. I was full of hope that my future in Dakar would be a great and fulfilling adventure into an unknown culture. But when I arrived here those hopes faded. This is just a continuation of a life I know so well, although the country and people are different. What did I expect? Something greater than India, a country that had captured my imagination.

(Tuesday 27 September)

The most exciting thing last week was the arrival of mail. What a relief! I was afraid it was being dropped into a dead letter box since we haven't recognized Senegal and theoretically our Embassy doesn't exist. But now we are legal, we've recognized Senegal.

This evening Mary, an Administrative officer, gave a dinner party to introduce her French friends. She is one of the older women in the Embassy and not very attractive, but she makes her life interesting by entertaining. A great part of the evening was spent eating and drinking. She is great at mixing up strange cocktails and food. The Menu: First course; cold crabmeat mixed with mayonnaise and brandy. Second; African dish of chicken in creamed peanut sauce over rice. Third; another African dish (equally as heavy) of fish in a tomato sauce over another kind of rice. Fourth; salad. Fifth course; three kinds of cheese with bread and butter. Sixth; fruit. Seventh and last course; rum cake with homemade ice-cream and creme de menthe liquor poured over it.

By this time one of the guests was violently ill and had to leave the party. I didn't feel well either and was glad when coffee was served and we could all go home. By this time my ability to speak French had about run out. It was a good experience and I was grateful to the hostess for taking on such an endeavor. Two guests, a French navel officer and his wife, invited the hostess and me to their house for dinner next week. Although they spoke French throughout the evening, they had been posted to a military airfield in Kansas and spoke English. They have just been transferred here and because of the heat, left their children in France.

(Wednesday night 28 September)

For the first time in my life I feel absolutely unnecessary to anyone or anything. Each night, after work, I come back to my small hotel room, take out my typewriter and write letters to friends, but I fear that my letters are "downers" and add nothing to their lives. I have reached an all-time low point and can't seem to pull myself together. I am completely disenchanted, and yet I haven't given up hope that this is the usual period of adjustment and will soon pass. Dakar has possibilities. Beautiful beaches, good horseback riding, tennis golf and the nights are magic, but oh, so lonely and empty without the right people. Learning the French language might be my only accomplishment here.

(Sunday 2 October)

Thursday I worked late into the night and got a rash on the back of my neck. Friday American Pat was feeling lonely so I went out to dinner with her. Interesting to discover her feelings; loneliness, boredom, dislike of her job and the country. Above all, disappointment in her first post. She wants the same things all women do, companionship, love and fun. She is a sociable person, witty and a good actress.

Saturday morning she went with me to see my new villa apartment about which my attitude is slowly changing. Who knows it might bring happy memories as did my "Castles" in Tehran and New Delhi. Will Ernst ever see it, or will I find someone to take his place? With my luck he'll never see it and there'll be no one to take his place. I have a distinct premonition that my place in his life has been taken by someone much like me, because I sense that he acquired a taste for a strong, independent woman who needs only his love and companionship, his greatest gifts. How do I feel about it? He is not right for me, but I would be sorry to lose him. He is a 'free spirit' and that's what attracts me. Seeing him here would be like the blissful trips we took together throughout India and later in Spain and France . . . far away from reality, where we were the only ones in the world. Would it begin all over again, or would I be able to accept the happy moments and then relinquish him forever?

Often I think of all the wonderful possibilities of being in love in Dakar. Sunsets, full moons. I must not think of that full moon in India on a hot night two years ago when Ernst and I slept on *charpois* on the guest house verandah near the famous Ellora and Ajunta caves.

(Monday 3 October)

It will be another week before I can move into my villa apartment. I mistakenly chose a whitish—pink paint for the walls, which turned out to be a sickening, shocking pink. I demanded that it be repainted pale gray, the color I wanted in the first place, but the owner had talked me out of it. They love violent colors. I dread moving, because I know there will be a hundred flaws to be worked out. I will have to hire a servant to tide me over until mine comes in December. At least I will have hot water to bathe in.

(Tuesday 4 October)

It's a beautiful morning. The sky still bears traces of night, and I'm sure if I walked out on my balcony, I would find that the full moon has not yet disappeared. Soon the tall white buildings, scattered between my hotel and the sea, will catch the rays of the early morning sun. Below me and across the street is a semicircle two-story building which houses some of the French Army. The flag has just been raised and the soldiers are moving around. The only noise is the call of the sea gulls; it is yet too early for traffic noises. The cathedral bells have long ago called out to the devoted. I can imagine there are a few Africans and Europeans scattered within the church saying their prayers, while Moslems, in other sections of the city are prostrating themselves on their prayer rugs, facing East.

And so another day in Dakar begins, fresh with the sea breeze and filled with the hopes and prayers of the faithful. For me it will be another day like yesterday and the day before, drowned in work from beginning to end, with the knowledge that I must continue being patient. This is only the beginning. Soon I will know more people and surely I can find some who bring joy and animation into my surroundings, and before long I can move into my apartment and surround myself with my books and souvenirs. After October is over and the heat subsides, I can drive my little car into the bush and get a glimpse of the real Africa. And I even dare hope to find a companion with whom to share the miles of beautiful white beaches, along which I have had the pleasure of riding a horse. And perhaps even someone to show me the city and islands from a sailboat and dance with me at the African night club, high on the water's edge.

In the streets I see such variety of faces, pure Negroid, mulatto, Moorish and sometimes an almost perfect black Jewish face. Tall men in long, flowing robes (*boubous*) stroll along the street with an air of elegance. Beautiful women seem to glide along like mannequins in colorful long flowing robes, with the left shoulder bare in the style of the French Empire. The material always looks too delicate for everyday wear; blue, pink, yellow chiffons shot through with gold or silver threads over an underrobe of colorful flowers or big dots. They wind the same material around their heads in beehive turbans. I wonder how they keep their robes clean. They look too delicate to wash and I don't remember seeing a dry-cleaning shop. The French people, especially now during the *hivernage*, fade in comparison. Perhaps it is the climate or just the general appearance of the "Colon". In Africa where one expects sparsely clad natives, it is just the opposite here. The natives are covered from neck to ankle while the white people are dressed in short shorts. The men in loose shirts and the women in strapless tops.

The center of Dakar is small, everything seems to be within walking distance, except the really good beaches. There are a few decent places to get a meal. Practically everything is imported and expensive. The cinemas show old French films. One can hear the sound of tom-toms in the distance at night, but otherwise 'Africa' seems far away. Since the black face is already familiar, I don't feel the "foreignness" here that I usually feel in a new country. The French spoken here is difficult to understand, but it is not the usual "foreign" language of a new country. One thing I do feel is the seemingly absence of any form of hostility on the part of the Africans toward the white man. The people are not servile. Why should they be? It's their country. They are neither resentful, nor cocky, as are the black people in the States, but here there are no signs "White People Only".

Working conditions, an integral part of my life, are not the best. We are crowded into what was meant to be a large apartment on the second floor of a rather nice building right on the main square. The personnel are of the usual consistency; married couples, a couple of bachelors (technicians) and many single women ranging in age from 24 to 45. The majority of the people have recently arrived and due to the housing shortage, are unhappy and frustrated, especially the single women, none of whom speaks French.

(Saturday 8 October)

Today I moved into my new villa—apartment on the first floor of an old colonial house with front and back walled garden. I can park my little car on the broad sidewalk in front of my house and enter the front garden through a metal gate. Once inside the gate a flagstone walk leads to a short flight of wooden steps. At the top is a wooden door in the green latticework that closes off the entire front porch. On the porch, to the left, is the toilet. The bathroom is reached by going through another front door, a large living room, a hall and up a short flight of steps which ends at the bathroom door. At least the flat is large with a living-dining room and two bedrooms, a primitive kitchen with a granite sink and a cold-water tap, and a pantry. There is one closet, the one I had made out of an alcove in the living room. The floors are marble and the walls are now a soft dove gray with white trim. The front and back walled gardens give privacy.

(Sunday 9 October)

First day in my new villa apartment. The woman who has been using my refrigerator damaged it and now it has to be repaired. I have no gas for my stove. The workmen are still milling about and I had to hire a "boy" to stay with the house during the day while I work.

This morning I ironed a dress on the bed and heated water for Nescafe on a hot plate from the office. By the time I got dressed I was drenched with perspiration from the stifling heat. All ready I'm discouraged with the whole idea of having my own place. Yet I know that I will get settled for the first time in over a year.

(Thursday 13 October)

Instead of sitting in a tiny hotel room, looking out at a 14-story skyscraper, I'm sitting at a desk in my barren study. Beside me is a bookcase and behind me a chaise longue. Through the open doorway I see my little back garden, shady and cool. The hibiscus bush is in bloom and the purple bougainvillea needs pruning. How lovely it would be if there was a bit of grass, but I have become accustomed to gardens without grass. Any minute now the bell will ring and I will run out to my front gate and welcome the African boy I have hired to stay in the house until the workmen have finished. He is supposed to do house cleaning, but this place is so old one can hardly tell when the floors have been cleaned. It took him almost one whole day just to clean the bathroom. Moving was the nightmare I expected. My fridge is still at the shop being repaired.

(Saturday 15 October)

This has been a maddening week. Worked at the office until one and two o'clock in the mornings preparing reports for visitors from Headquarters. In the midst of it all my car broke down and is in the garage being repaired. My boss has assigned me to entertain the visitors from Washington. They arrive tomorrow. I will drive them into the countryside and along the beach about a hundred miles, lunch at a seaside restaurant, back to Dakar and a ferry over to the Isle of Gorée to see where slaves were held before being shipped off to America.

(Wednesday 19 October)

Last night I took the visitors to see African dances. By the look of the all-Senegalese audience, I would say that this was authentic Senegalese music and dance. The women wore matching bras and sarongs, which made it seem staged for

European audiences. Yet in one of the wild, stomping, whirling dances a live chicken was sacrificed on the stage. This caused some squirming among the visitors. They leave tomorrow for Bamako, giving me a chance to catch up on my backlog before they return.

(Saturday 22 October)

Our Ambassador arrived yesterday with an entourage from the State Department. There will be a reception for him this evening, after a big luncheon party for the visitors this afternoon. One of the visitors is the Deputy Secretary of State who was Ambassador to Iran when I was there and remembers me.

(Sunday 23 October)

I now have my fridge and can enjoy a cold drink. The house looks barren. My household effects are on their way from India. I borrowed an ironing board and ironed until midnight.

(Tuesday 25 October)

Now that our Ambassador has arrived the Embassy is in turmoil because there is no space. We are on top of one another, frustrated and bad tempered. No immediate relief in sight. Office space in Dakar is at a premium. I guess we'll have to build a chancery. We have a new Ambassador's residence, which is sort of jazzy and completely out of keeping with gracious Ambassadorial living.

Today the diplomatic bag from Bamako brought me a letter from one of the Headquarters VIPs. He thanked me for making his stay in Dakar so pleasant and hoped we could have more time together when he returned from Bamako. Something about the letter made me a bit uneasy. I had noticed that he was constantly at my side.

(Thursday 27 October)

My secret admirer arrived from Bamako yesterday morning. After a lovely day and evening together I drove him to the airport this morning. He is a widower, nineteen years my senior, very young looking, energetic and in good health. He wanted to have me transferred back to Washington where we could get to know one another and let time decide if age difference mattered. I was tempted and in months to come I might regret refusing his proposal. I felt sad on the way back from the airport.

The rest of the sweltering day, in an office without air conditioning, seemed endless. The dense atmosphere, like a fuzzy woolen blanket, muted street noises from below. Perspiration trickled down my chest, irritating my prickly heat rash and soaking my bra and panties. Heavy with fatigue from lack of sleep and mesmerized by the droning, overhead fan, I kept nodding off. Mercifully, seven o'clock finally released me.

Sleep was the only thing on my mind as I drove my little gray *deux chevaux* home. I pulled up on the sidewalk in front of my bougainvillea-covered wall and, with rest in sight, I plodded to the garden gate.

It was locked.

I rang the bell. No reply. I gazed forlornly through the metal bars. Darkness. Not a sign of life. How had this happened? I went back over the events of the day.

I had awakened to a crumpled dress on the chair, blue pumps in middle of the floor. Burned-out cigarette in the ash tray. Necklace and bracelet, my admirer's gift, on the table.

I had struggled into a cotton dress, hoping there would be time for a cup of coffee before my French teacher arrived. No such luck. The garden gate bell sent me trudging out the front door, across the lattice-enclosed porch, down a few steps and across the garden flagstone path to open the gate.

"Bonjour Mademoiselle," my teacher, a stern-faced Frenchwoman, smelling of garlic, greeted me seriously. We sat at

the glass-top dining table and I repeated after her: *"Le plus que parfait. J'avais aime, tu avais aime, il avait aime, nous avions aime . . ."*

Finally the lesson ended and the teacher left, unhappy with my lack of progress.

I headed for the kitchen, gasping for caffeine.

The sudden jangle of the garden gate bell stopped me in my tracks. I turned on my heel, stormed out of the house, down the flagstone path and threw open the gate, ready to say, "Go away."

There in front of me stood a tall, grinning Senegalese man in a red fez and an orange *boubou*. Before I could say my piece and slam the gate, he informed me that he was the replacement for the "boy" I had employed to clean the house and stay until I returned home after work.

I couldn't imagine this elegant man cleaning my house, but he seemed eager to get started. I showed him the broom, mop, scrub bucket, laundry soap, iron and ironing board. He said he could iron, but seemed a bit puzzled when I took a rolled towel from the fridge, unrolled it and produced a damp cotton dress to be ironed. I'd put it there to avoid mildew because I didn't have time to iron it.

All hope for a shot of caffeine had vanished.

On leaving I gave him the key to the garden gate and told him, *"Fermez bien la porte du jardin. Attends moi ici parce que je ne que'une clef."* I spoke slowly and repeated, keep the garden gate locked and wait here for me, because this is the only key I have. All the while he grinned and nodded his head, causing the tassel on his red fez to swing back and forth.

Now, ten hours later, I find that he obeyed my order to lock the gate, but he'd missed the point. "Stay until I return," I had repeated, "because this is the only key I have."

I took one last, forlorn look at the dark house, wearily turned away, drove to the Embassy and called the three decent hotels in town. Nothing available. I went back to my house, hoping the 'orange boubou' man had just gone out for some local food.

No such luck. The gate was still locked and the house dark.

I didn't even know his name, much less where he lived. My feet hurt and my head ached and I had lost my sense of humor. I berated myself for not having a spare key, but that only increased my headache.

At my wit's end, I was staring through the shadows in the garden to the green latticework door, willing it to open, when I heard an African voice from out of the darkness.

"Are you looking for M'dou?" A skinny man in a blue boubou, who could have been my temporary boy's older brother, stepped into the street light.

"Yes," I said, without even knowing if that was, indeed, my temporary boy's name. "Do you know him?"

"*Oui.*" He grinned as though he knew a secret and eagerly nodded his head, covered with a wool skullcap.

"Where does he live?"

By his furrowed brow I could see that he was having just as much trouble understanding my French as I was his.

"I will take you there." His wide smile, full of strong white teeth, indicated that he was happy to share his secret.

The first thing I knew I was driving toward the Medina, native district, with my ill-smelling "angel" leaning over my shoulder from the back seat.

"To the left,' he directed. "Now to the right. Stop here. Ici!"

He crawled from the back seat, unfolded his thin, supple body and sauntered into the village of small shops and shabby houses, honeycombed with dark alleys. In the dim lights of the huts, I could see him shaking hands with all the villagers, exchanging pleasantries.

The hours of sleep, I had promised myself, diminished with each handshake, each peal of laughter, each slap on the back. When he disappeared down a dark alley, I went into my defense mode; I put myself into neutral while onlookers strolled by, taking a quick second glance at my white face.

And then, at last, from out of the labyrinth of dark alleys, my grinning orange boubou "boy" came loping toward me. With a thousand apologies he handed me the key to my garden gate.

On the way home I thought how nice it would be to arrive and find the house clean and all my cotton dresses washed and ironed and hanging in the closet.

With the garden gate firmly locked behind me, my thirst drove me straight to the fridge. I threw open the door, expecting to see coca colas. Instead the shelves were neatly stacked with rolled towels containing all my still-damp freshly-washed dresses.

I howled with laughter, drank a warm coke, went to bed and slept soundly.

(Friday 28 October)

I woke up this morning with a sore throat. It had been sore for a couple of days but I have been too preoccupied to notice. I have just come from the doctor, who said I had a slight infection of the larynx. He advised me to give up smoking and stay out of *"le courant d'air"*. As though anyone could stay out of *a current of air* in Dakar and survive the intense heat. He gave me a powder. I'm to put it into a great bowl of boiling water, then hold my head over the bowl with a towel, covering it like a tent, and inhale. Too complicated. Besides I don't have a great bowl. Together with the powder, he gave me an ill-smelling liquid I am supposed to *"se gargariser la gorge,"* and a pile of suppositories. The French depend on suppositories for everything that ails them.

(Saturday 29 October)

My 7:30 a.m. French lesson was interrupted by the door bell. I rushed out, unlocked the gate, threw it open an found a strange African standing there. I was about to send him away when he told me he was the gardener a friend had promised to send. So there went precious time explaining to him, after my French teacher left, what should be done in the garden, as though I knew.

(Sunday 30 October)

This morning I feel cornered, rebellious and in an anti-people mood. I haven't had time to get acquainted with my new "home" much less enjoy it. My last three weekends were taken up by chores. The first I moved into my house and spent Saturday and Sunday unpacking, scrubbing and doing laundry; the second weekend I took Washington VIPs into the countryside to see the "bush." Last weekend my opposite number in the British Embassy was feeling depressed, so I devoted my day to taking her about fifty miles into the countryside for lunch at a lovely place in the orange groves. By the time we got to the beach the day was almost over. Again no suntan. Today I will take some of the girls to the beach, because I'm the only woman in the embassy who has a car.

(Monday 31 October)

I can tell my diary about all my activities, except my work. A secrecy agreement deprives me of this liberty. My work consumes most of my waking hours and my energy. In my past Embassy posts, I managed long, stressful hours of work more easily because I had an exciting personal life, which I don't have here. I'm trying to be calm and optimistic, but my patience is growing weak and I'm tired of trying. I have lost my enthusiasm and I no longer respond to the comforting cliché, "that everything is going to be all right." Even so, I know that I will go on and I know that I will make some sort of a compromise, beginning with my work. I must lower my standards and cease even attempting to be a perfectionist. And, above all, I must do it in a way which will not effect my own personal sense of duty. I have never attempted this before because I am so self-controlled that I'm afraid that if

I let down on one front, I might give in all together. I have let duty to work assume too much importance, and neglected duty to myself. I was brought up to do my chores first and then I would be free to do pleasurable things. This is a good rule, when there is time for both. But struggle as I do I never finish my chores. So I try to do everything and am constantly frustrated and resentful, especially toward people who mean very little to me, or I to them. They take precious moments I have saved either for myself or those who really mean something to me. I have become so rebellious that I now declare periodic days of silence.

Today my boss, who doesn't value time as I do, spent the whole afternoon discussing my "attitude". He said it was cold and hostile and would have to change if things were to work smoothly. I totally agreed and tried to get on with my work. I even told him that my resentful attitude was in part caused by having to work at night because of constant interruptions during the day by his friends who come to "shoot the breeze". I was disappointed that he didn't understand and offer to limit such interruptions. After stealing my afternoon talking about my "attitude", with which I agreed from the onset and promised to try harder to be more sociable, he left at five for a cocktail party, and I stayed on, working into the night.

(Tuesday 1 November)

Today was one of the many local religious holidays. I refused to go to the beach because I didn't want to see anyone. I worked late last night so that I could have the entire day to myself. But before the day was half over one of the girls in the office dropped by and brought me a garden hose. That was O.K. But now I've just received a call from the Boss. I have to go to the office, after four, to encode and send out a message and then tonight I have to make a "contact".

Having twenty-four hours to myself seems impossible. I get so fed up with people that I sometimes can't bear to hear a human voice. (Reading this over, I see how weak I am. I can't say "No" and then I blame everyone who takes my time. Either say "No", or shut up complaining.)

It is almost four o'clock. My time is up. What did I do with the day? Got up at seven (the mornings are a bit cooler) ate some bread, butter and jam and with my coffee I wrote to Maya, my Indian friend. Then I re-ironed a cotton dress; my part-time servant is hopeless when it comes to ironing. I spent a couple of hours putting my papers in order and making out a list of letters owed, things to buy for the house, things that needed doing. After my friend left me the garden hose I watered the garden, cleaned off the paint on the trees and walkway. I then cooked myself a big bowl of rice, which I gulped down and now have the stomach ache. All in all, I do feel better having had at least these few hours in my house. Now I must go to the office.

(LATER)

Every time I go to the Embassy on Sunday, or a holiday, I marvel at the ease with which I enter. I go through a side entrance, next to the shipping office on the ground floor, walk up a dark flight of stairs to the second floor, take out my key and unlock the door. No fortified door, no dead bolts, no Marine guards, just a simple key. Other foreign diplomatic posts where I've worked, with the exception of our Consulate in Lahore, Pakistan, have been heavily guarded by U.S. Marines. They checked the identity of each person entering and leaving.

Easy access to the Embassy and the lack of security amazes me. A few days ago, hidden behind a pile of file folders on my desk, I was engrossed in encoding a secret message. Suddenly I became aware of a shadow falling across my encoded message. I whirled around in my swivel chair and there standing on the balcony was a grinning young Senegalese window washer. I hastily grabbed file folders and covered the code book and waited patiently for him to finish washing the French door windows. At least, I comforted myself, the doors were closed. I've had to keep them closed for the past month, and forego the ocean breeze, because sudden gusts of wind blow secret papers onto the balcony. In the past I've retrieved them before they sailed out over the railing.

But I wasn't so lucky when I was burning secret trash on the roof of the American Consulate in Lahore (Pakistan). There, too, I was under cover as a Consular clerk which meant that I really shouldn't even have had secret trash. Little if anything in the Consular Section is classified. So as not to blow my cover I waited until the Consulate closed at one thirty for lunch. Then, with the 'burn bag' in hand, I headed for the roof where the Embassy burned its secret papers in a large mesh cylinder suspended above the roof. A small opening on top allowed papers to be fed to the flames.

One day, while feeding Secret papers to the flame inside the mesh cage, I was idly gazing across ugly rooftops at barren, dry landscape and thinking about my peanut butter sandwich for lunch. I was pulling a handful of papers from the bag when a sudden wind gust snatched them and sent them flying across the roof. I chased after them and managed to retrieve a few before they went over the edge. Helpless, I watched the others float down into the street.

Leaving the smoldering secret trash, a security violation, I grabbed the burn bag and flew down the steps shouting for Sandra, the only other person on duty in the Consulate.

She rushed out of her office wide eyed. I told her what had happened as I shoved the secret trash bag in my safe. She was not CIA and shouldn't have seen our documents, but I was desperate for her help.

We ran out into the street. Thank God it was siesta. There wasn't a soul to watch us, two tall fair-skinned women in high heels, scampering about, chasing paper. To this day I will never know if we retrieved every single sheet of paper marked 'Secret'.

(Friday 4 November)

Today the Embassy receptionist, Madame Brie, called me and said, "Mamadou is here to see you." It took me a moment to realize that Mamadou was, I hoped, going to be my new servant. Soon after I arrived in Dakar I had solicited Mme Brie's help in finding a good servant. She recommended Mamadou, saying that he was an excellent cook and would be free the first of December when his 'Master', a French bachelor, returned to France. And now the moment had come to meet him.

I arrived at the reception desk unprepared for the scene before me. Mamadou looked more like an African King than a servant. With a dark-red fez perched jauntily on his head he appeared to be six and a half feet tall. His dazzling-white damask robe fell from powerful shoulders to within inches of the floor. Strong black hands, protruding from wide sleeves, hung limply at his side. Tribal scars marked his dignified, unsmiling face, yet in his intelligent dark eyes there was a hint of suppressed mirth.

As I approached he took a step forward and greeted me in French. Returning his greeting, I realized I couldn't possibly ask such an imposing figure to do my laundry, especially my undies. I turned to Madame Brie and asked her to conduct the interview.

He didn't flinch when she told him that I expected him to do laundry. After he agreed on a salary and assured us that he could iron a cotton dress, even one with a pleated skirt, he fidgeted as though we were wasting his time with foolish questions.

"Have you ever worked for a woman?" Madame Brie asked.

His broad face broke into a wide, white grin, showing a slight gap between two large front teeth. "No," he lowered his head, chuckling, "but I'm willing to try." He spoke directly to the receptionist as though I didn't know what they were saying. "I have heard Americans are nice people to work for," he added.

He repeated the directions to my house, at No 8 Avenue Roosevelt, said he would report for duty at seven o'clock the first of December, bowed and swept out the door, probably with a sigh of relief.

(Sunday 6 November)

A nice quiet day, getting tanned. Most of the day I spent lying on a mattress under an umbrella reading about the *Mundugumor* tribe in New Guinea, whose social structure is built on hostility rather than love. Quite a contrast. A man is considered maladjusted and a misfit in the society if he: takes care of his family, including his mother-in-law; is kind to his own son; does not sleep with his own daughter, or trade her off for another wife for himself. A woman is a misfit if she is plump and soft, refuses to throw away her first child, is maternal, good natured and devoted. But in the end, like most societies, they formed alliances for the sake of killing the "enemy".

(Monday 14 November)

Each morning I wake up to the sound of the sea, which is in back of my house, but invisible because of my garden wall and the huge trees in the neighbor's overgrown colonial garden. The nights are cool now and I can open my window.

(Wednesday 16 November)

I came home for lunch today. Still don't have my cook so I had cheese, wine and yogurt. My house is lovely during the day; cool and quiet and clean and spacious. With the green shutters closed against the midday sun I can barely hear the birds singing in my garden. Although my house faces a busy street, there is no noise at the moment. Everything stops between noon and three o'clock. We have a two-hour lunch break, during which I usually eat a heavy meal at a cheap restaurant (even so, it's about $1.50!) and then return to the office and work the second hour. When my cook comes to prepare a big lunch (Oh, happy day!) I might learn to take a siesta, but I'll always write in my diary with my after-lunch cigarette as I'm doing now.

(Friday 18 November)

After two months I finally succeeded in prying loose, from the customs, my record player. I remembered taking it to the Embassy in Paris where I was promised that it would be properly crated and shipped to me in Dakar.

And now, with excitement, I watched it being uncrated, recalling how I had tried it out in my artist friend's Left-Bank loft and anticipated the joy, and sorrow, of hearing my Indian records again.

While still lost in these thoughts, I watched the box I had delivered to the Embassy being lifted out of the crate. When it emerged I gasped with horror. One side, right through to the bottom, had been smashed in. The damage had been done by the French packers before they had wrapped the box in waterproofing paper. And they had the nerve to send it on without even trying to hide the fact that they had done the damage! They had even trimmed away the ragged ends of the paper in which I had wrapped the box before they crated it! I went raging into the Embassy administrative office, demanding an explanation. I was told that the embassy would pay for having it fixed. Afterwards, I realized that letting this unimportant event grow out of proportion was one of the tragedies of my empty life.

(Saturday 19 November)

The sun is about to break through. (It is still dark here at 0630.) As soon as the traffic noises begin I will know it's time to get up. An ideal morning, cool and fresh; a summer dressing gown can be worn in comfort. I'm sitting at my dining room table, black wrought iron with a glass top, looking through the big, old fashioned windows onto the back garden. Another day and another chance to be "human" is mine and I shall make the best of it. I slept very well, after an exhilarating horseback ride late yesterday afternoon.

It was pitch dark when I got back from the stables after a canter along the beach with British Pat. I almost fell asleep during dinner. Once in bed my eyes stayed open long enough to read only a few pages of *Sex and Temperament*—I'm on a Margaret Mead jag. She studied four societies in New Guinea. One in which men and women worked harmoniously around a structure of quality and cooperation with no strict dividing line between sexes; another society built upon hate and violence and aggressiveness; another in which the men took the lead because they provided the food; and the fourth in which the women provided the food and were the strength around which the society was formed. The men were the artists and their sole purpose was to entertain the women and build their ceremonial houses, into which women were not allowed. In none of these societies was there any emphasis upon behavior being related to sex; such as boys must be strong and aggressive and girls must be weak and submissive. Mead came to the conclusion that temperament was not based on sex but on the social structure. The Western, so-called, civilization being the most difficult of them all. There were a few misfits in all these societies, but nothing to compare with the number in our harsh and inhuman "civilized" society.

(Monday 21 November)

Needing to mail a letter yesterday (Sunday) I drove out to the airport. No stamps. I returned to the Embassy and scrounged enough postage for a letter to France. By this time it was seven o'clock in the evening and dark. The Post Office was on a one way street, going in the opposite direction, so I parked my car on a slight incline and started around the corner to the P.O. On the way I was stopped by a night watchman who, seeing the letter in my hand, told me the P.O. was closed.

While talking to him I heard a loud BANG. We both ran around the corner. To my horror my little *Deux Cheveaux* was lodged up against the curb, halfway down the hill. Ahead of it another *Deux Cheveaux* was rolling happily down he street, driverless, out of control and headed for a car parked on the opposite side.

We both started running to stop it. We got there just at the moment it collided, but the combined weight of our bodies hurled against the car, softened the blow. There we were, holding the little gray car back with our bodies and torn between laughter and fear that the owner would appear on the scene.

We managed to push it back across the street, but we couldn't get it up the hill from where it had come, after my car had hit it. I got in and parked it, and then stood there laughing with the night watchman, thinking what a funny sight it must have been to see us running (I in high-heeled sandals) down the street and throwing ourselves in the pathway of a car. What did the owner think when he found his car parked in a different spot from where he'd left it?

(Wednesday 23 November)

African dances by the Jeuness Catholic. I wasn't keen on going, afraid they would be sterile with missionary influence. On the contrary. They were the best I've seen so far; a wildly primitive mass of male and female bodies, arms and legs, whirling and stomping in gay abandon. A girl lost her bra, but didn't miss a step. They seemed to be under a spell of ecstasy. Their infectious gaiety, their technique in performing difficult acrobatic movements demonstrated their ability to display a more profound self-expression than the usual monotonous feet-pounding dances. Their costumes, if not authentic, were good imitations.

One girl was wearing a sarong made of material with two huge pictures of President Senghor on it, one centered in the front of her skirt and one centered in the back. I got so carried away with Senghor's facial expressions as she gyrated her hips that I wasn't aware of the other dancers. The audience, including some pale-faced White Fathers and Sisters (nuns) in their yellowed white robes, was enthusiastic. They were more sophisticated than the usual audiences of mothers in native dress with their baby strapped to their back, or hanging on their breast, and restless children climbing about, all of which I missed at this performance.

(Thursday 24 November)

Ever since I got my little car, with canvas hammock seats, I noticed that the engine spurted hot air on the passenger's side. When friends complained of the heat on their feet I just passed it off as normal in such a hot climate. But when my friend's dog refused to ride in the front seat, I decided to see if anything could be done.

I took the car to a service station and asked the Senegalese attendant to have a look at it. He peered under the panel and, with a puzzled expression, shook his head. He didn't seem to have a clue. Luckily a curious Frenchman standing nearby offered to help. I told him the problem. He reached under the dash and pushed a lever.

"Madame," he addressed me with disdain, "why do you keep your heater on in summer? Isn't Africa hot enough for you?"

(Saturday 26 November)

My boss and I have talked about my transferring to another post because my working habits don't meld with his. I work hard eight hours a day and don't think I should come in on Saturdays and Sundays. He, on the other hand, fools away his time and then comes in on Saturday to do what he should have done during the week, which means I have to come in to do the typing and code work. We have agreed that I will stay a year and if by that time we decide we are not a good team I will transfer.

As I write this I know that it's mainly my attitude. My boss is a kind and very sociable person, well liked by his colleagues. He has a Latin concept of time, except when the diplomatic pouch goes out and then at the last minute he works furiously to make the deadline. I, on the other hand, have the old Anglo-Saxon work ethic and slog steady all day, believing that the office is a place to work not socialize. So I resent having to work overtime to get the diplomatic pouch out. My free time is all I have to cling to, and I don't want it taken away from me.

(Monday 28 November)

Today I was allowed to go along on the U. S. Military Attaché's plane to pick up our Ambassador in Nouakchott, where he had attended the Mauritanian independence celebrations. The flight to the capital, Nouakchott, was one hour and forty-five minutes.

We flew low along the coast, passing over St.Louis, the main part of which, much to my surprise, is built on an island at the mouth of a river. The contrast of the blue water, white sand and gray desert was fascinating from five-thousand feet up, but I imagined that it might be dull to drive along the makeshift road; a trip I had originally wanted to do, but now I am not sure would be worthwhile.

We landed in the dust and confusion of departing dignitaries. I was surprised to see the majority of them wearing overcoats.

But when I stepped out of the plane I knew why. The early morning desert air was cool. The Ambassador, though eager to return to Dakar, kindly let us have his car and chauffeur to take us to see the plot of barren earth, where someday the American Embassy would rise, and then on to the new section of town.

White and pink government houses rose majestically against a cobalt-blue sky in the middle of a wide expanse of nothingness. Where else would you find government housing with plumbing tested by international dignitaries? Including the young Agha Khan, looking very handsome in a dark suit.

The most interesting sight was at the airport where the Blue Tribes had been assembled to entertain the guests with music and dancing. A marvelous sight and one I'm sure I'll never see again, even if I went there to stay for awhile. I was surrounded by a group of women, tattooed around the mouth, some playing stringed instruments and others giggling behind makeshift veils. Their facial features were coarse and heavy, while the men had thin, aesthetic faces.

(Wednesday 30 November)

Yesterday morning I went out in my back garden to take in my clothes, washed the day before by my part-time boy and still hanging on the line. At the bottom of the steps I almost collided with a strange African man washing his clothes in my outdoor laundry basin. We exchanged greetings. He didn't seem at all disturbed and continued scrubbing his long cotton robe, which had turned the water, in the concrete tub, a deep blue. At least he had brought along his own laundry soap. I took my clothes from the line and curious as to who he was and how he got into my private garden, I asked if he were a neighbor. He said "No", adding that he was one of the men who had painted the house next door. We said our farewell and I went to market, berating myself all the way for not asking him to explain how he got into my garden.

When I returned he was gone, but from my clothes lines

hung strange garments, tunics, boubous, Arabian-nights trousers and small things I didn't recognize.

Later I went to the Embassy to send out a telegram and when I came back the clothes were gone. I hope he didn't feel slighted because I hadn't made available my ironing facilities. In poor countries one gets used to such happenings and learns to accept them.

Once on a visit to the Taj Mahal I witnessed a little brown Indian man strip down to his loin cloth and wash his clothes in the reflecting pool. Seemingly unaware of all the tourists streaming by, he scrubbed his *dhoti* and shirt, rinsed them and then laid them out on the grass to dry while he took a nap in the shade.

(Thursday 1 December)

Mamadou arrived this morning at seven. I showed him the kitchen, which had only the basic equipment . . . a couple of cooking pots and a butcher knife. Seeing the disappointment on his face I explained that my household effects from my last post, India, would arrive soon and there would be plenty of kitchen equipment. By the look of relief on his face, I imagined that this promise had produced visions of all sorts of modern American gadgets. I'm afraid he will be disappointed. My cook in India needed only the basics to produce delicious food.

When I came home for lunch Mamadou served the fish course and then disappeared. I sat patiently at the table until my curiosity sent me to the silent kitchen to see what had happened. Through the open door I saw Mamadou in the garden, prostrate on his prayer rug, facing Mecca. From then on, I came to lunch at one o'clock.

(Monday 5 December)

Although Mamadou is now my cook, I still get my breakfast. He doesn't think it's civilized to serve breakfast at 0630 hours, so he doesn't arrive until a few minutes before I go to work. I'm not pushing him. This would be one reason to let him go after his trial month. The laws are very strict here; if you fire a servant, you have to give him one month's salary. That is, if you keep him past the month trial period. Mamadou wants $48.00 per month. Most people pay only $36.00. He is an excellent cook, but I can see he doesn't like housework. (Oh, to have my Indian servants.)

(Tuesday 6 December)

Today I came home for lunch and found Mamadou, standing just inside the door, grinning. After he greeted me, he turned slowly around, like a model, showing me his new uniform; royal-blue Arabian-nights trousers and a knee-length white tunic with a square neck and long loose sleeves. When I pointed to his bare feet he said he didn't want to wear shoes in the house. I didn't insist.

(Wednesday 7 December)

A gin/tonic and two glasses of wine at a lunch party left me drowsy all afternoon. I quit work an hour early, dressed in riding clothes, and collected my teenage riding mate, Alice. When we started riding a few weeks ago she was very shy and unsure of herself, but now she is more open and self-assured. She tends to be a bit pudgy, but in her new riding clothes she looks smart. She was happy with her new black velvet jockey cap like mine.

We planned to have a jumping lesson at the beach academy, but the instructor didn't come. We were glad and instead had a long gallop along the water's edge. Alice's horse started acting up so we decided to return to the stables.

Riding along the beach at water's edge we were enjoying the cool wind, off the raging sea, and the beautiful red sunset spread across the water as it washed up on the shore. Further out the pale green water broke into white-capped waves and further at the horizon it was almost black. In the gathering darkness the fishermen had just brought in their catch. The beach was crowded with people, in native flowing robes, amidst piles of fish.

As we started across the sand dunes, turning away from the sea toward the black outlines of village huts, my horse broke into a gallop. Alice's stallion came racing after my mare. We finally got them calmed down, when all of a sudden her horse lay down and started rolling in the sand. She jumped off before he crushed her. But she couldn't get back on because the horse was out of control and finally tore the reins from her hands. The next thing I knew he was stampeding toward my horse. I tried to keep her reined in and calm, while lashing out with my riding crop to keep the attacking stallion at bay. But when the stallion tried to mount her I got my feet out of the stirrups just as my horse bucked and I slid off the back, landing on my tail bone. Fear paralyzed me. Would the rearing, battling horses trample me to death as I lay there with pain shooting up my back. Finally they turned, still fighting, and disappeared into the semi-darkness over the sand dunes.

Alice, only 14, was trembling when she came to help me to my feet and held my arm as we headed across the cooling sand dunes to the stables. The fishermen had come running to help us, but there was nothing they could do. We thanked them and trudged on.

Before long we heard a vehicle's engine and voices coming through the dark. It was the stable owner driving his truck with a search party in the back. We almost fell into one another's arms with relief.

"Thank God," he said in French, "when the riderless horses galloped into the stables, I feared I'd find both of you lying, wounded, somewhere on the dark beach."

(Thursday 8 December)

My household effects from India have arrived at the port. The dreaded moment of finality has arrived. I loathe unpacking my past and being reminded in a thousand ways that my dream to give up this life has not come true and that the possibilities grow smaller each day. Most of all, I will be reminded of what an excellent servant Ram was, compared to my new servant, who is a good cook but cares little for housework and has no imagination or charm; two attributes which can make me forget the dusty corners and half-finished laundry.

Once the crates are delivered, unpacked and placed around me I will be trapped again. I will be past the point of no return. I can no longer fool myself by thinking this is only temporary and that if I'm patient it will all end. In reality this is the beginning of a new chapter. I hope I can muster up enough enthusiasm to make it a memorable period of my life.

(Friday 9 December)

While having lunch today my gaze wandered through the big window into the garden. There on the clothesline hung my panties and half-slips. The elastic of each piece stretched to the limit between two clothespins and for good measure two or three in between. This is hard on underwear which can't be replaced here. But the formality of my relationship with Mamadou makes it very uncomfortable to show him the proper way to hang out my undies. I was glad he didn't lay them on the ground as is the African custom. I find it difficult to criticize a six-foot-three-inch man who looks like an African king with tribal scars on his handsome face. He knows his duties and does them well, except cleaning house and hanging up my underwear.

(Sunday 11 December)

It's a lovely, cool morning. A bright sun sheds heat rays from the royal-blue sky. I have locked my garden gate and shut all the big green shutters over the front windows, closing myself into my villa apartment. It's my day of silence. I need to gather my thoughts as I sit at my glass-top dining table before a half-finished

Christmas card list. The only sound is Bach's B Minor Mass from the record player.

(Next Day)

After the last sentence the garden gate bell interrupted me. I let it ring, but after a minute of insistent high-decibel buzzing I knew it must be important. Reluctantly breaking my silence I stormed out and threw open the gate.

It was my boss.

"There's a woman at the Grand Hotel looking for you. She arrived from Pairs on the 4:00 o'clock plane this morning." He mispronounced her name and I didn't recognize it.

I was just about to say that I didn't know who she was when it dawned on me that it was Magda Liguori, my Argentinean artist friend. She'd arrive in Paris a few days ago and I didn't expect her for another week. I thanked him. I was in need of a friend.

Soon she and her luggage settled comfortably in my spare room. She hadn't changed much. Her black hair was still short and curly, her dark, penetrating eyes sparkled with joy, the sun had bronzed her pale skin and, as always, she wore no makeup. But she seemed shorter. I always towered over her, but now she seems no more than five two, but still a strong character and creative in painting, writing, and poetry.

We talked for hours. So much had happened to both of us since we parted in New Delhi over a year ago. She had traveled in the Orient, painting and giving art exhibits along the way. She had even painted Indonesian President Sukarno's portrait. She fell in love with Bali and stayed there until her sandals wore out and she had to spend her precious money for a proper pair of shoes to wear to Paris. She's still a free spirit.

(Saturday 24 December)

Magda and I play scrabble in French, a neutral language. It's all very well for her. She can spend hours during the day studying French scrabble words while I deaden my brain with routine office work. She always wins and it frustrates me. How ironic it will be if my household effects are delivered while she is here. She was with me when they were packed in New Delhi. At the time we had speculated, over and over again, "Where would I see them again?" We thought of many exotic places, but never Dakar, Senegal, French West Africa. I'd never even heard of the place. Nor did we ever imagine that Magda would be with me when I saw them again.

(Thursday 29 December)

Magda and I passed a pleasant Christmas. The day before we drove into the countryside and had a big lunch at a French restaurant by the sea and later slept it off in comfy beach chairs in the shade of acacia trees. Christmas eve we opened our presents. With her last penny she had bought me a big art book, "*Sculpture Africaine*' illustrating sculpture throughout Africa. I gave her a sweater I'd had sent out from the States. She had no warm clothes. Christmas day we had dinner with my boss and his family. Monday after Christmas was a holiday and we spent the entire day talking. I'm getting rested up for our trip to Portuguese Guinea this weekend.

**My little *Deux Chevaux* car in front of the garden gate
at No. 8 Roosevelt Avenue [Dakar 1960]**

My front garden [Dakar 1960]

My porch entrance into house [Dakar 1960]

With Magda Ligouri on the N'gor beach [Dakar 1961]

PART II

1961

(Saturday 31 December 1960 to Wednesday 4 January 1961)

Early this morning, like two thieves, we crept out of the house before first light and silently closed the garden gate behind us.

In semidarkness the macadam road into the East Lay silent and black through the parched landscape. Etched against the sky ancient Baobab trees, their massive roots and trunks with spindly, barren limbs, are doomed to be naked forever in dry desert air from the north and torrential summer rains. Legend has it that God was angry because they wouldn't grow where he wanted them, so he tore them up and stuffed them back upside down. Some are over 2,000 years old. They grow quite rapidly for the first 250 years. Most are hollow.

We drove along the shore where sea gulls frolicked on the white sandy beach. Soon the fishermen would arrive with their early-morning catch, pull their boats up on the beach amidst a crowd waiting to buy fresh fish. Now and then, as we approached a roadside village of round thatched huts, tall, black figures in long, flowing robes, appeared on the road, moving slowly in some direction of meaning to them. At one village a quick glance through an opening in the spiked-wood fence revealed a bare-breasted old women drawing water from the well, Dreaming, perhaps, of her youth at that very spot.

Out of the silence of the vast space ahead came light and

noise. The first town emerged as a silhouette against the pink and orange dawn. The pale-gray massive cement factory spewed forth dark smoke against the rising sun. Figures passing between us and the rising sun were like lantern slides of Balinese puppets. Birds, in groups, flew out to sea.

We settled back into the surrounding silence, thinking of the long trip ahead to Portuguese Guinea and how good a cup of coffee would taste. We had prepared everything for the trip; a borrowed ten-year-old road map, films for the movie camera, champagne for midnight. The brakes had been tightened and the engine purred smoothly. All was well, or was it? Why was the car slowing down? Why has it stopped? Out of gasoline? Couldn't be. It was filled only a few days ago. But how many days? I couldn't remember.

I grabbed the measuring stick from under the seat, jumped out, unscrewed the gas tank cap, and plunged the stick into the tank. It was dry! We were dead in our tracks only one hour and forty miles from Dakar.

Magda, who knows nothing about cars, volunteered to go to the nearest gas station with and old white-faced settler, who stopped to help us. Silently cursing myself for not filling the tank, I watched her climb into the settler's rickety commercial van and disappear in the direction we'd come. Pacing back and forth on the narrow strip of macadam, I had begun to worry when a shiny new car, driven by a glamorous French woman, arrived with Magda and a tin of gas.

Magda told me how she'd tried, in her Spanish-accented broken French, to explain our predicament to the Senegalese gas station attendant. She said he had suppressed a smile when she told him we were on our way to Portuguese Guinea and had run out of gas. By her description and hand gestures of the car's size, and the fact she was wearing slacks, the local natives, who had gathered around her, decided she must be traveling on a motorcycle. The attendant gave her three litres of gas to get her to the next station.

They hadn't yet recovered from this strange woman's sudden appearance when we arrived to return the tin container. I had the tank filled, not daring to go on to the next station, which might not have petrol.

From then on I did my penance by stopping at every gas station. Sometimes there was an ancient hand pump, but mostly there were roadside shacks selling gas from five-gallon tins. No matter how primitive and how little bit of gas I needed I kept the tank filled.

The extra time we'd had at dawn had slowly run out and there was a long line when we arrived at the ferry between Senegal and British Gambia. The map showed that Gambia was only a strip of land, divided by the Gambia River, wedged into Senegal, like a hot-dog in a bun.

We watched the ferry chug back and forth across the Gambia River, loaded with human beings and their status symbols of success and prosperity; shiny new bicycles, transistor radios and European clothes, mostly hats. Hats of all descriptions: knitted wool toboggans to protect their shaved heads against the burning sun; red fezzes as a badge of their belief; the British-introduced tope, some still in cellophane wrappers; rakish berets, almost covering one eye in the French style; felt fedoras with wide brims (twenty years out of style). A few cowboy hats, tied under the chin, proudly displayed MEXICO in large white letters across the front; bright-yellow baseball caps advertised Gulf Oil. Even karakul hats that made the cold winters of Russia seem far away and unreal. Old Ghurka army hats, symbol of younger and more exciting days of retired British sergeants, now in the African colonial service.

On and on they poured onto the ferry that would take them closer to families, awaiting their return from the harvest of the north. After each ferry load departed, silence descended and the faces around us became as flat and immobile as the landscape under the midday sun.

A friendly Gambian customs official, in traditional wide-legged

British Army shorts, with a swagger stick under his arm, approached our car after studying the Senegalese Diplomatic license plate.

"Vous ete en promenade?" he said in excruciating French. When we confirmed we were, indeed, on a "stroll" he asked for our passports.

Seeing that I was an American, his face lit up and a broad, white grin spread across his shiny-black, round face.

"Ah," he said to me in British-accented English, "My American cousin!" He came to attention, clicked his heels, saluted and said in a military tone of voice: "At your service good lady," followed by a gush of English. "How far are you motoring, good lady?"

"Portuguese Guinea."

"You have commenced at Dakar?"

"Yes."

"Your good husband is awaiting you in Guinea?"

"No."

"Oh, I see," he said slowly as though he really didn't understand, "you are just taking a stroll for the holidays." with that he signaled that our little car was to be put on the ferry. The captain said there wasn't room, but the policeman motioned me to cross the ramp and ordered room to be made. In the end they had to lift my little gray car into an empty space. All the way to the next shore the muddy river seemed to be flowing sideways.

We drove off the ferry and barreled down the dusty, unpaved road. As we rounded a curve a lopsided truck, listing under a heavy load, was coming straight at us. The driver kept waving us to get out of his way.

"He's going to hit us!" Magda cried out, gripping the dashboard.

"Monster!" I said, turning the car down the embankment to avoid being hit.

It wasn't until we met another heavily-loaded truck, coming straight at us, with the driver waving his arm out the window, that it dawned on us. British Gambians drive on the left-hand side of the road.

As we entered Bathurst, the capital, a cricket match was in full swing. It could have been a scene in an English village. The players, in immaculate whites, stood out on a bright green cricket pitch. But there was something different. All the faces were black. The colonized had adopted their colonizer's favorite pastime.

I knew we would have to enter Senegal again before reaching Portuguese Guinea, but there were no road signs. How would I know where to switch from left to right-hand side? I approached each curve with fear, not knowing which country I was in. Luckily the only time I came face to face with another truck I had enough time to shift sides before colliding.

After many tense miles we came to the Senegal customs officials. We were completely lost and thought we had arrived at the Portuguese border, but when the customs officer started complaining of his liver (*foie*) I knew we were back in French Senegal, where the natives had taken on the French malady of liver trouble.

When we entered the rice-growing Casamance region the road turned from black asphalt to red clay. A fine, red powder trailed each movement on the road's surface and tinted the green trees and fields a soft pink. After miles of this rough, corrugated road, we came upon a sign reading: *Chaussée déformée* (deformed road) and the thin ridges in the road turned to small mounds of pavement spread over nature. As though the sign post had been invented at this very place, we found all sorts of signs pointing out roads and crossroads that weren't marked on our ancient map.

It was growing late, but we rolled on, lost and thirsting to death with only a bottle of warm champagne to celebrate the new year. Finally we arrived at the seaport city of Ziguinchor.

The sun was sinking and we were still two hours from the Portuguese Guinea border. What to do? Turn inland again through the thickening jungle inhabited by the Floups (once cannibals

I'd been told)? We decided to stay, but soon found the only European hotel was already filled with colons on a "stroll" for the holidays. We thought of going on, but as the narrow, dark roadway, carved out of the jungle ahead, became more vivid in our imagination, we chose an African hotel, a picture of tropical decay, green paint peeling, broken windows.

We persuaded the hotel keeper, who never took off his felt fedora, even while making the bed, to change the sheets on the bed for a set that looked a bit cleaner.

Later at an oilcloth-covered table in the city's only European restaurant we joined the scattering of solitary "colons" glumly eating their New Year's eve meal. Occasionally they glanced or simply stared, as we did, at the boisterous French couples celebrating at the tiny bar in the corner. The ladies sat on high stools and the men hovered over them, retrieving their drinks from the bar. This, we assumed, was the local French colon society's smart set, self-assured in their homemade finery and cheap jewelry.

A baby cried and we all looked around, suddenly conscious of one another. A tiny infant, only a few weeks old, lay on its mother's lap. The young mother's big, brown eyes, deeply set in a pale, drawn face seemed dull and unfocused as though the effort of giving birth had exhausted her. She pacified the baby and everyone became self-conscious all over again, each group modifying its former activities. The noisy bar patrons became a bit quieter and the solemn couples spoke a few words to one another.

We'd all settled back into finishing our meal when a dog, the sole companion of an old woman huddled over her soup, started howling at the full moon, shining through the open door.

We could no longer bear the depressing scene. We downed the last bit of wine, paid the bill and left. This was not the way we had wanted to spend New Year's Eve.

Back at our sleazy hotel we opened the warm champagne, afraid we'd fall asleep before midnight. We were weary after a long day and a bottle of wine at dinner had made us drowsy. In the silence we sipped champagne from a paper cup and stared out the dirty window screen. In the bright light of a full moon my little car, sitting all alone, looked so vulnerable in the big empty space between the hotel and the dark forest beyond.

Before we finished the champagne, distant tom-toms called from deep inside the forest.

"Let's go!" Magda downed her champagne and jumped up.

"I don't think we should," I said, hesitantly.

"Isn't that what this trip is all about? To experience Africa."

"Of course!" I said, remembering the first time I heard the tom-toms after I arrived in Dakar and how, without thinking, I had jumped up from my desk and rushed out on the balcony to see the tribes celebrating in the square below. Since then I have heard the drums late at night and wondered what it would be like to go into the bush and watch the ritual. Now was my chance.

"Let's go!" I threw the rest of the warm champagne down the cracked sink. "The tom-toms are calling."

We left through the back door, ran past my little car and into the forest. As we slowed to let our eyes adjust to the dark we got a fix on the direction from which the drumming came. When the haunting sound of the tom-toms grew louder we slowed to a cautious walk. The soft ground muffled our footsteps as we approached a clearing in the forest.

There, spotlighted by the full moon, drummers in loin cloths, their faces painted white with black vertical slashes down the cheeks. Their drums slung around their necks, they beat out a steady, monotonous rhythm, while men in haystack masks, a spear in their right hand, moved in a slow dance. Lined up, facing one another at a short distance, the dancers swayed forward, closing the gap between them, clashed their spears and then swayed back. To the beat of the tom-toms their feet stomped the powdery earth, raising little clouds of gray dust. The drums beat faster and faster and the bare feet pounded the earth with fury. They plunged toward one another, whacked their sticks against their opponents, and then backed off. Tension heightened. Finally, in a crescendo of high—pitched wailing, they broke ranks and whirled, like dervishes, as though in a trance.

Fascinated, we inched nearer. Suddenly a voice cried out and one of the drummers pointed in our direction.

"Let's get our of here," Magda, the brave one, whispered.

We ran blindly, afraid to look back. Finally, out of breath, we stopped behind a tree to rest. Then cautiously we peered around to see if we were being followed. Not a shadow moved under the tall trees.

"Which way did we come?" I whispered, looking ahead, hoping to see light from the hotel.

"I don't know, but we'd better keep going."

In spite of the stitch in my side I ran after her. We heard a dog howling and went in that direction, hoping it would be the dog at our hotel.

It was. Crouched in the hotel doorway it wouldn't let us pass. Every time we moved toward the door it bared its teeth and lunged at us. We called for help, but all we got was silence.

Terrified of dogs we gave up easily and ran for the safety of our car. There, curled up in the uncomfortable canvas hammock seats, we passed from 1960 to 1961.

After a breakfast of bread and coffee, we gladly left Zigenchour and headed for Portuguese Guinea.

At the border we were not welcomed. The officials didn't like the idea of two women traveling alone and tried to persuade us to turn back, but we stood our ground and finally after half an hour, uncomfortable in our presence, they let us pass.

We were nervous as we drove through the region inhabited by a tribe that once delighted in human flesh. But the old men working in the fields, whether clad in a loin cloth, or loosely hanging Western clothes, bowed, curtsied, waved or tipped a real or imaginary hat and smiled. The women, naked to the waist and carrying their baby on their hips, or strapped on their backs, stopped their work in the rice fields and waved. Younger men, some wearing sarongs of bright-colored homespun cloth and others in odd and unmatched African or European style clothes, saluted with their long, shiny-bladed machetes. We wondered if any among them had ever tasted human flesh.

Further into the jungle we encountered a band of young men. Clad only in brief loincloths, they wore necklaces of teeth or amulets, stark white on their black skin patterned by scarification and carried bows and arrows. They surrounded our little defenseless car. Magda, completely unafraid, opened the sun roof and, standing on the unsteady canvas seat, captured the moment on movie film. I gripped the wheel, terrified that I would hit one of them, and waited tensely to press the accelerator the minute they moved from the front of the car. When they realized Magda was pointing a black box toward them they stopped running beside the car. Maybe they thought it was a gun of some sort. In any case I pushed the accelerator to a dangerous speed on the narrow, dirt road.

"Fantastic!" she cried. "We got a movie,"

"And survived," I added, but I expected an arrow to come whizzing through the car's canvas top at any minute.

This fear soon faded into another tense moment. I suddenly came face to face with a dark stream in the dense jungle. The only way across was a bridge made of two logs set the right distance apart to accommodate the wheels of a car. The skin on my face tightened and my mouth went dry. Were there alligators in that dark water waiting for my little car to slide off the logs and sink into their territory?

I slammed on the brakes and slid frighteningly close to the stream's edge. Then, with trembling knees, I got out and tried to judge whether or not my wheels would be the right width to fit on the logs.

"What do you think?" I asked Magda, the happy-go-lucky Latin, and already knew her optimistic answer.

"Looks good to me," she said, glancing from the logs to the car wheels and with that she danced across on one of the logs. "*No es problema!*" she called out from the other side. "I'll guide you onto the bridge."

That was no consolation. I gripped the wheel and prayed all the way across. Once safely on the other side I suddenly thought, "I'll have to do this again in a couple of days," and wished I'd turned around and aborted the trip. It was too late now.

I didn't relax my hold on the steering wheel until I saw the beach at Varela, glistening white in the midday sun, inhabited only by shells and driftwood. Beyond, the blue Atlantic merged into the sky. We had reached our destination.

Lunch on the patio, perched near the edge of a cliff high above the Atlantic, was Portuguese and heavy. The thick dark red wine and the sound of waves, crashing against the base of the cliff made us sleepy. We giggled nervously about our escape from the tribes as we climbed the hill to our little cabin in the pine forest. It was dark and cool, inviting us to a siesta.

Later, as the sun was setting we ran down to the sea. The water was cold and bracing. The sand, still warm from its long exposure to the sun, clung to our wet bodies.

Dinner on the cliff patio underneath colored lights strung from the vine trellis, hanging with bunches of small, green grapes, was some sort of a heavy meat stew with hunks of dark bread. Good with hearty red wine. Dessert was a compote of figs. Not the best of food, but the ambiance was exotic. We were the only guests and got a lot of attention, even though we had to communicate in sign language and Spanish of which a word now and then sounds like Portuguese.

Added to the wind murmuring in the pines and waves crashing against the cliff came the primitive beat of the tom-toms from somewhere in the surrounding jungle. I went to sleep imagining the dark, shiny bodies swaying as their naked feet rose and fell against the jungle floor, warding off evil spirits.

A typical African village in the bush [Senegal 1961]

Senagalese village women [Senegal 1961]

Senagalese village women [Senegal 1961]

A typical village market [Senegal 1961]

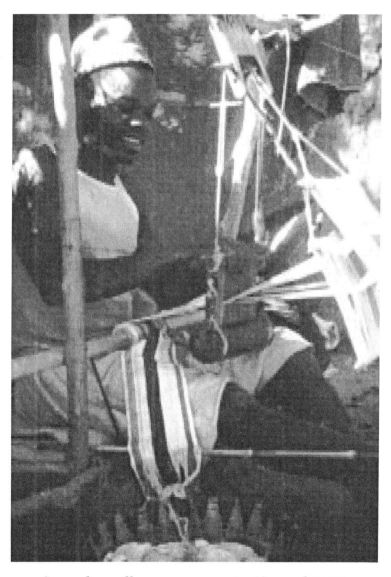

Senagalese village woman weaving [Senegal 1961]

Senagalese village children washing cooking pots
in the river [Senegal 1961]

The President's Palace [Dakar 1960]

(Wednesday 6 Jan)

Back in Dakar. Today I was coming home to lunch, an hour late as usual, agitated because my boss wasted all morning yaking with a friend and then gave me a telegram to send out at the last minute. He went home to lunch while I encoded the message and took it to the post office to be sent.

As I approached my house, I gave a left hand signal, intending to cut across the road and pull up onto the sidewalk in front of my gate. As I turned I heard a crunching noise and felt my door caving in, pushing my seat sideways. My car slued around, barely missed an oncoming vehicle, ran up on the sidewalk and hit a tree. Stunned, I got out to see what had hit me.

There on the street sprawled a French soldier, his face bleeding where he had hit the pavement. Nearby lay his Vespa motor scooter, the wheels still spinning in the air. I was terrified.

I thought I'd killed him. Before I could call for help, a French doctor, living in the house next to mine, came running out. I wanted to go help the soldier, who by this time was sitting up, but the doctor quickly summed up the situation and hurried me into his house. After settling me in a comfortable chair he called the military ambulance to take the soldier to the hospital. I felt responsible and wanted to go with the ambulance. But he cautioned me that it was unwise for me to get involved.

"The laws here are tricky." he warned me. "You'd better write out a description of what happened so you can tell the police when they come." He gave me a sheet of paper and a pen and insisted that I drink a glass of brandy to quieten my nerves.

When the Police came they could see I was in no condition to be interviewed in French. They told me to return to my house and they would come to me when I felt better. The doctor escorted me to my house.

As we approached, I could see Magda and my cook standing in front of the open garden gate staring at my car lodged up against a tree on the sidewalk. The driver's door was smashed in and the fender badly bent. When they turned and looked in my direction their eyes widened as though seeing a ghost.

"What happened?" Magda ran and threw her arms around me. "We heard the ambulance as it was leaving and came out to see what was going on." She released me and looked me up and down as though making sure I wasn't wounded. "We saw your car and thought you had been taken to the hospital, badly wounded." She hugged me again.

(Sunday 15 Jan)

My dreams last night were filled with sounds and scenes of the motor scooter hitting my car. In one dream a soldier came bursting through the window at eye level and in another a bloody man lay dead on the street, his open eyes staring accusingly up at me. I woke before dawn in a cold sweat, concerned about the poor soldier even though the doctor assured me that he would be all right.

Magda's time with me is up. She has been here over a month. I have "grown accustomed to her face" and having her around the house, especially at meal times. Together we have discovered the pure pleasure of eating. Mamadou is an excellent cook who delights in stuffing us with delicate and beautifully prepared food. We can hardly wait until meal times and then we sit at the table, moaning and groaning with delight at every bite, praising the French for their contribution to epicurism. Here's what we ate for Magda's last dinner with me . . .

— One dozen each of oysters on the half shell
— Veal scaloppini with cream potatoes that made us sigh with each bite.
— Bottle of white Bordeaux wine
— Watercress salad (a separate course here)
— Camembert cheese (one of our passions) with crusty French bread and butter.
— Bottle of good Burgundy wine.
— A bowl of fresh fruit: oranges, tangerines, apples, bananas
— Chocolate mousse
— Coffee.

All this after a full four-course lunch!

Magda's plane to Buenos Aires was scheduled to leave at 2:30 a.m. Just after midnight we left the house, having nothing more to say, and drove out to the airport, along the dark cliff-side road.

She didn't want to go. After a year of freedom, she now has to make a decision; will she sacrifice everything to become a recognized artist, or will she give up that dream for financial comfort? I rather think she will choose the former, but it will be a hard road. While here with me she didn't paint at all, but taught

me to make monocopies and left me her paints. She did write
one short story and finished another for me to translate from
Spanish.

(Wednesday 18 January)

My recent admirer sent a telegram with love for Christmas
and another for New Years. I don't expect to hear from him often,
or for a long period of time. The age difference is too great, but
meeting him was a lovely interlude.

Ernst has disappeared. Magda saw him in Paris and said
he'd had a bad business break and was depressed. I'm not
surprised. Like all my lovers, he is an artist and not a business
man. Born into a noble Scandinavian family he never learned
how to earn money.

(Thursday 17 January)

Today the French police came to the Embassy to interview
me about my car accident. My boss, who knows the officer, acted
as interpreter and did most of the talking. The French soldier,
who had completely recovered, said that I didn't give a left-hand
signal. My boss stood up for me and declared that it was my word
against his. Because of the friendship between my boss and the
police officer, I felt pretty sure I'd win the case when it came to
court.

(Friday 20 January)

My trunks from the States arrived yesterday. I've unpacked
my records and at the moment I'm listening to Mendelssohn's
concerto in E Minor for Violin and Orchestra. I still don't feel
strong enough to listen to my Indian records. Too many memories
of Ernst.

Just after my record player was repaired Mamadou watched

out of the corner of his eye as I put records on the turntable. Obviously he expected to hear American music. Instead, when I settled the needle on the record, African drums blared forth. He stopped dead in his tracks and looked at the record player as though it was some strange spirit. I quickly explained that I have liked African music for a long time. He smiled. Later, when he served dinner and noticed I wasn't eating much, he said in French, "You miss your friend."

(Sunday 22 January)

Determined to have a whole day of silence, I locked my garden gate, put Bach's B-Minor Mass on the record player and took out the oil paints Magda left. The day flew as I made monocopies as she had taught me.

I painted African masks on a pane of glass and pressed normal typing paper on the painting to make copies. Then I placed each sheet on the marble floor to dry. To keep the sheet from curling up I anchored it with seashells, knives and forks and spoons, ash trays. Anything heavy enough to keep the wet pages flat.

Soon I got bored with small prints and decided to make an enormous one on the glass-top table. With bright paints I made a long stick figure with a big mask for a head. I had just enough brown wrapping paper to run off two copies.

I got so carried away I forgot the time. Before I could clean up the mess Mamadou came to prepare dinner. I thought he would be furious for having to clean the paint off the dining table. Instead he seemed more interested in the African paintings, spread out all over the floor.

Carefully, tiptoeing on bare feet in the space between drying monocopies, he gazed down and shaking his head, he mumbled, "*Pas mal, pas mal.*" 'Not bad' was a compliment coming from him.

My day of silence has rid me of anxiety brought on by pressure and a sense of not wanting to be here. I feel calm inside now and I have taken time to enjoy the beautiful day outside. A bluer sky

I have never seen and softer breeze I have never felt. I kept thinking of the beach, but knew that I must first settle the storm inside me. And now I feel mentally and physically exhausted. I'm emotionally wrung out by Bach's Mass, played over and over until the music penetrated my whole being and sent my emotions from depression to euphoria. I am ready now to continue making this new life a great experience.

(Monday 23 January)

I'm having some African University students, all girls, in for tea this afternoon. It is hard to entertain without proper dishes, but I'm tired of waiting for my household effects to come from my last post in India. Getting to know Africans is more important. Very few are included in diplomatic affairs, but that is bound to change now that the French are leaving. I have been going to the English Club at the University to talk with the students, but having them to tea is a better way to get acquainted.

(Tuesday 24 January)

Last week the Embassy was notified that I would have to appear in court for causing an accident on 6 January. I chose a plain dress, well down below my knees, remembering my court case in Turkey in 1950 when my apartment in Ankara had been burgled and a cuckoo clock stolen. Turkey being a police state the culprit was soon caught and no doubt "pressured" into confessing. A Turkish lawyer, working in the American Embassy, went with me to court. I was wearing a navy-blue blazer, red cashmere sweater, white skirt, blue stockings and red high-heeled platform shoes. We appeared before the judge. In the background I could hear the culprit's poor peasant family sobbing quietly. And in the docket was a pathetic young man with a black eye. I told my lawyer to tell the judge that I didn't want to press charges. He looked at me as though I were an idiot and denied my wish.

Before the proceedings started the judge whispered something to the clerk of court, and the proceedings stopped until the clerk fetched a chair from behind the scenes and brought it to me. A courtesy to a foreign guest in his country. He returned to his place beside the bench and the proceedings started. Halfway through the charges I automatically crossed my legs. The judge stopped his discourse, whispered something to the clerk of court, who came to my lawyer and whispered to him. My lawyer bent over and said, "Uncross your legs. The judge is about to charge you for trying to influence the court in your favor." (Not surprising since Turkish women have been liberated from the veil for only twenty-seven years.) I got my cuckoo clock back, but at the price of that poor man serving time in a Turkish jail. When I left Turkey I gave the clock to my servant.

So here in Senegal I carefully chose a simple dress and appeared, with an Embassy officer, in front of the judge. (Unlike Turkey I wasn't offered the privilege of sitting down.) It turned out to be a routine automobile accident case. The French sergeant, whose motorcycle struck my car, smiled at me when I entered the courtroom. He admitted that I had given a signal, but at the last moment, leaving him no time to react. I was fined about a $100.00 to compensate for repair to his Vespa motor scooter, which seemed fair to me. I wanted to apologize to the sergeant, but my council advised against it.

(Monday 30 January)

The report that my household effects had arrived from India was false. Now I hear they are nearing Dakar. They were put on a ship that didn't even stop in Dakar and had to be transshipped.

(Thursday 2 February)

Last night when Mamadou served my dinner with a big grin on his face it took a moment to realize he was wearing sunglasses.

As he stood there grinning I noticed the sticker price still on a corner of the right lense. He was very proud of his new status symbol, which I'm sure cost him most of his last month's salary. I felt like giving him a lecture on wasting his money, but then remembered that sunglasses, here in Africa, symbolize success. So I grinned back and said how well he had chosen.

(Sunday 5 February)

I feel surprisingly well after dancing until six o'clock this morning. My African university friends took American Pat and me out on the town. She is resigning. She hates Dakar and is disillusioned with the Foreign Service.

My University friends, from leading Dakar families, are not allowed to go out, even with me, without parental approval. They are Moslems. They don't smoke and drink nothing stronger than coca cola. We went to the N'Gor Hotel to dance and when the orchestra stopped playing at 0230 hours we went on to the best night club in town which caters to the young smart set, black and white.

The Senegalese are wonderful dancers and were patient enough to teach me the cha cha cha. It was interesting to look out from the dance floor at the white people, sitting at surrounding tables. The French didn't even seem to notice our white faces among all the blacks on the dance floor, but I caught some Americans I knew staring at us and whispering among themselves. Not only was the dancing tiring but having to speak French and translate for Pat for eight hours "wore me out".

(Wednesday 8 February)

I hate myself! Today I had an opportunity to talk about my problems to an official from Washington and I blew it. I blurted out a lot of nonsense, as one does when everything is penned up and festering inside. I'm sure I sounded like a frustrated old maid, whose whole life is taken up with small, unimportant things. I know I left a bad impression. Sadly I didn't have a chance to recoup before he left. I can only hope that he was a bit sympathetic to my position. The damage has been done, but I hope I have learned a lesson I thought I already knew; never complain to someone in high places about your boss. I found out long ago that they all stick together, while brushing me off with "she's probably going through the change." At least I promised the VIP that I would either conform to the existing work pattern, or resign.

(Saturday 11 February)

Yesterday Mrs. B, the French receptionist, called and said a young French woman was there and wanted to exchange French conversation for English. "I called you, Mademoiselle, because I know you are eager to learn our language." I agreed to see her although I didn't want to get involved with yet another person to gobble up my precious time.

In her late twenties, Jacqueline, was a bit nervous and shy. She is a pretty woman, slim with dark hair and pale complexion and sad, dark-brown eyes. After only a few minutes of speaking English I could see that she was really looking for a big sister to hear her woes. Someone to lean on. She told me that her husband was Algerian and that she was on a French Government contract to teach in the local African school. I really didn't want to commit myself, but her sad eyes persuaded me (the big sister of the world), so I asked her to tea the following week.

(MONDAY 13 February)

My household effects from India finally arrived last week. A lift van (metal box) about the size of a small bathroom, was unloaded on the sidewalk in front of my house. Too big to get through the garden gate, it was left on the wide sidewalk, where curious African neighbors gathered and pedestrians paused to stare and comment. Prolonging their curiosity, it remained there, waiting for the keys to unlock it.

Meanwhile, Mamadou packed up the borrowed pots, pans, dishes and glasses, obviously looking forward to a better supply from the mysterious metal container in front of the house. Today three men from the moving company arrived with the keys and the unpacking began.

Passersby, dark-eyed school girls their hair in tiny braids, women in colorful, gauzy, flowing boubous with one shoulder bare and their heads wrapped in matching turbans, old men in white caftans, serious young men in business suits and an occasional vendor, with his wares, sweets or fruits, piled on a tray balanced on his head, gathered and watched. Unfortunately there wasn't much to see. Everything inside the metal container was packed in boxes and wrapped in brown paper. The boxes and bundles were carried inside the garden and eventually to the front porch where they were unpacked under Mamadou's supervision.

Bed linen, books, paintings, old letters, old clothes, glasses, dishes, furniture were unpacked and taken inside the house. Mamadou showed interest only in the abstract paintings. He stared, tilted his head from side to side as though trying to figure out what was in the picture.

While the last crate was being pried open I suddenly remembered that I had given all my kitchen equipment to my Indian cook, but I didn't have the heart to tell Mamadou.

By midmorning the unpackers had gone and the porch was empty except for a pile of clothes and bedding I'd given to Mamadou and a box marked "Miscellaneous." I left him to open the box and went inside. When I returned I got as far as the front door and stopped.

Mamadou, standing on the porch beside the open box, had donned a maharajah's shiny gold brocade turban from the box. In his hands he held a gourd flute, which had once belonged to an Hindu snake charmer, a friend of mine. Cautiously, he put the flute to his lips. As his cheeks puffed out a sudden shrill note broke the silence. He jerked his head back and glanced furtively over his shoulder. Seeing me, he quickly put the flute down and started to remove the turban.

"*C'est à vous*," I said, "and the flute is yours too."

A broad grin lit his face and the joy in his eyes was that of a boy with a new toy. He hadn't noticed there were no fancy American kitchen gadgets, much to my relief. Tomorrow I will take him shopping for what he needs.

(Tuesday 14 February)

Today my French protégé came to tea and told me her life's story: On a holiday in Algeria she met a young man from Tunis. After a short courtship he wanted to marry her. Her parents objected, but she went against their wishes. Since then she has been teaching in French colonies and recently was posted to Dakar. She said that she gives her salary to her husband, who doesn't have a job. As her confidence in me strengthened, she told me that he locks her in their little house in the African section (Medina) on weekends, without money, and goes out on the town. When I asked her why she stays with such a dreadful person, she says, "I'm afraid of being alone. If I divorce him I may never find anyone else to marry me and I would grow old alone."

I pointed out that she couldn't be more alone than she is now; at least she would be free to have a social life. But she is fixated on the idea of being married. She has found out he has a mistress and wants me to find a handsome Frenchman to take her out dancing to make her husband jealous! I can feel myself getting deep into her life without the courage to say "NO!"

American Pat, who resigned, now finds she doesn't have enough money for transportation home and will have to stay until Next April. She is miserable and I'm the only who cares. Then there is British Pat who can't bear being alone for a moment and I'm the only one who will tolerate her and her big dog, who digs up everything in my garden when she brings him here. All this crying on my shoulder saps my energy and patience. I grew tired of being mother confessor years ago and no longer consider it flattering, when my friends come to me for counseling. Mostly they are just plain selfish and have no consideration for me. They have no real interest in me as a human being with problems. Their eyes glaze over when I suggest that I, too, have problems.

I'm getting a bit hardened to these intruders in my life, but I'm still a pushover. Why? Because I'm genuinely interested in human relationships. The more I learn the more I mature and the more I mature the better prepared I am to live this sort of life, completely on my own. No one there when I come home at night. No one to be concerned if I don't come home. No one beside my bed when I'm sick. No one to cheer me up when I'm depressed. By helping others I become stronger in coping with my own problems.

At least I've learned to announce that I'm having a weekend of silence and am not available until Monday. But this doesn't prevent them coming by, ringing my garden gate bell until, thinking it's an emergency, I rush out, throw open the gate and find a familiar face and hear a little voice saying, "I thought you might be tired of being alone." Someday I'm going to have the courage to say, "I'm **never** tired of being alone."

After having said all this I have to confess that I asked Jacqueline to come to dinner tomorrow night and bring her husband. I can't believe I did it! I already dislike him, sight unseen.

(Wednesday 15 February)

The dinner this evening for Jacqueline was tedious. I even felt Mamadou's dislike for Ahmad, Jacqueline's husband. I couldn't believe that a cultured, traditional, attractive young French woman could have married such an uncouth man. He is dark, low forehead and stocky build. By European standards he has neither manners nor culture. That could be forgiven, because he is another culture, but he has no saving graces. There is no kindness in his dark, shifty eyes and cruel mouth. He has, naturally, an Arab man's viewpoint toward women; they exist to serve men. She can't tell me why she loves him, but she does and can't help it. I tried to hide my dislike, but I'm sure his animal instinct alerted him.

(Friday 17 February)

Today I wrote a letter to the kind Headquarters Inspector to whom I had poured out my heart. I told him that his visit helped me to see myself at the office and that I had changed my attitude and now there was complete harmony in the office. "This could not have happened without your help," I wrote. "I have discovered that I am working with the kind of boss I like as a human being."

(Sunday 19 February)

Yesterday I took some of the Embassy girls up to St.Louis (about 250 miles north). It is a charming city, built on an island in the mouth of the Senegal River and reminiscent of the New Orleans Latin quarter with wrought iron balconies and white houses covered in bougainvillea. A port city, developed by the French it, too, isn't the real Africa. We stayed overnight in a nice, old French hotel.

(Wednesday 22 February)

The Ambassador was very kind to invite me to his party for American VIPs: medical delegation, Inspectors and an Anthropologist from the Library of Congress. Their opposite numbers in the local government were invited, but few came and even fewer brought their wives. We have difficulty getting Local dignitaries to come to our receptions. Perhaps because before they were independent we were very cozy with the French. Now the French have gone and the Senegalese are not cozy with us. As a matter of fact when visiting VIPs want to meet young people I'm called on to give a lunch party and invite my university friends.

Haven't heard from Ernst. A friend in Paris said he'd gone to Finland, where he was born while his father was a Swedish diplomat there. Correspondence with my recent admirer is slowing. We both realize that our meeting was a lovely interlude in our lives and we will leave it at that.

(Friday 24 February)

Jacqueline now tells me that her husband is planning to leave her. He has packed his clothes. She is desperate. She loves him. His behavior is destroying her. Could she come spend the weekend with me? There goes my precious weekend. I had wanted to finish reading Ionesco's play, *Rhinoceros*, which I saw in Paris last year.

(Monday 27 February)

I'm too exhausted to write, but I mustn't let too many days pass. It's difficult to catch up.

Jacqueline talked nonstop from the moment I picked her up Saturday morning, took her to the beach and then lunch at the N'Gor Hotel. Double feature French films on Saturday night didn't quieten her. Now she says she will buy a car for her husband to keep him from leaving her. (Idiot!) I tried to tell her what a heel he is.

Soon after I took her home on Sunday and had settled down to answer my admirer's letter, I heard a loud banging on my gate (the bell doesn't work) and there was British Pat to tell me her problems, too mundane to record, but mainly about her boss. She should not be telling me anything about her boss, chief of British Intelligence in Dakar.

(Tuesday 28 February)

I haven't had the energy to sort out my household effects, which sit around in great lumps. I had grown used to living in an empty house. Now I feel crowded and wish my effects had ended up in the sea. I'd rather have the insurance money. I had planned to give a housewarming party, but it is Ramadan, the Moslem month of fasting (they don't swallow a single thing, even water, during daylight hours, but are allowed to eat after the sun goes down.) My poor cook, who is already irritable, certainly couldn't cope with a party. I will give it next month.

Since my French teacher returned to France in January I've been looking for a replacement. At last month's meeting of the University English-speaking Club I spotted a very slim, well-dressed, young Senegalese girl with a serious, intelligent face. I caught her eye, exchanged smiles and felt good vibrations. I approached her and after pleasant exchanges she accepted my invitation to my house for tea. Since then she has been coming every other afternoon at five for tea and French conversation. Her name is Aminata, but I call her Amy. She is a devout Moslem so now, during Ramadan, we postpone tea until the sun goes down in respect for her religion.

(Thursday 2 March)

When I'm invited to Amy's family and friends they are always surprised that I'm an American. They think all Americans hate blacks and certainly wouldn't associate with them. I want to prove that Americans are as democratic and human as **we** say we are. With the race riots going on in the States it will be hard to assure them, but if I can convince a few that we carry out our Christian practices, as **we** say we do, I will feel that I have not wasted my time. I've yet to live among more pleasant and friendlier people than the Senegalese.

A continuing thought: I want to quit work and go off to Paris after my year is up. If I don't make a break now I will have to wait until I'm fifty! The very idea depresses me. Giving up my job will not solve any problems, but at least I might stand a chance of finding an exciting companion in Europe. Yet it would be foolish to give up this comfortable life for an uncomfortable one somewhere else which might be even lonelier. At this moment I would say "yes" to my recent admirer, whose letters are endearing, but he said he was leaving all the moves up to me and I don't have the courage to write and tell him. Besides, I'm not sure I really want to marry. Underneath it all, I'm a loner at heart. A loner who would like a playmate.

(Friday 3 March)

It is a cold, dark morning. The wind whistles and waves beat against the sea wall. I love it! Jackie is losing her husband to a French house of prostitution where he spends most of his time. Her sense of humor saves her and makes it easier for me. She does make me laugh. She is a brave girl, hopelessly in love with her scoundrel husband, who treats her like Arab husbands treat their wives. Her latest idea is to get her husband back by having a baby. This time I minced no words. What a stupid idea, I told her. He will leave you the moment you can't support him and then you will be landed with a baby to care for. I suffer for her because she cannot cry.

Mamadou is feeling the effects of Ramadan. He is pale(!), moves slowly and is withdrawn during the half-day he is here. Amy, my French teacher, eats heartily of my bread and butter after the sun sets.

Surrounded by my effects from India I'm homesick for the life I had there. I really had an affinity for that country, its music and dancing and its people, literature and art. Ernst and Magda were part of that life.

Rather than try to rearrange my house to accommodate my copper and brass objects, Indian carved screens, paintings and souvenirs, I just sit at the dining table and paste photos in my album.

I have finished Japan, Turkey, Iran and Pakistan and started India. A wonderful means of escapism. Reminds me of a colleague in India who could never get around to putting her shoeboxes of photos into albums. One day when her man servant came to her and said he'd finished his work and had nothing to do, the idea struck her. She took from her closet arm loads of shoe boxes filled with photos. "Go to the market and buy pretty albums," she instructed him, "and then make me some nice picture books with these photos." I never saw the finished product, but I've tried to imagine how this illiterate Indian boy arranged those photos. I lost track after hearing that he was grouping the photos by matching the faces. Surely in the end she helped him. Otherwise she must have the most bizarre photo albums in existence.

I'm having stomach trouble and feel tired. The way I used to feel in India when I had amebic dysentery.

(Thursday 9 March)

I've been in bed for two days with temperature, sore throat, no appetite. This morning, feeling better, I asked Mamadou to bring my portable typewriter. He rolled his big dark eyes. He doesn't know that my typewriter is my companion. Most people have live companions, but I have only my keyboard to talk to.

I hate being sick. It hurts my feelings. I take it personally and all the suppressed self-pity comes crashing down on me and I dissolve into tears. But reading *Balthazar*, by Lawrence Durrell, is keeping my mind occupied. I usually make myself read French so this is a luxury.

The weather has been perfect for the past three months. I dread the hot weather, only a month away.

(Monday 13 March)

I have returned from a weekend in Bathurst, British Gambia, and have finished a bowl of the shredded wheat I bought there.

The French don't eat breakfast cereals. Having passed through Bathurst with Magda I really didn't want to go back, but I had promised American Pat that I would take her before she left Dakar.

The USIS Director, an elderly American bachelor born in Germany, went with us. He still has a heavy accent and tends to be a bit of an old maid. Rather than spoiling our trip, as we had feared, he turned out to be a good traveling companion and thank goodness he was along. A tire went flat just before we reached Dakar.

We left early Saturday morning and arrived in Bathurst after three o'clock in the afternoon..nearly 300 miles, of which about forty were not paved. Mercifully the weather was not very hot, overcast sky, dry and dusty countryside. Small thatched-hut villages dotted the landscape of tall brown grass and lots of big baobab trees. The Africans call them upside-down trees because the barren limb look like roots.

The ferry across the Gambia River, which practically cuts Bathurst off from the mainland, was crowded. I got a dent in my fender trying to fit my car into a small space. The ancient ferry takes only one truck at a time, but we managed to get my car aboard. Having diplomatic license helped. Otherwise we would have waited hours because there was already a long line of trucks when we arrived at the ferry. But this time I didn't see the border police officer, who had called me his 'American cousin', when Magda and I passed through after Christmas.

Bathurst is a small town, surrounded by water on three sides with a few nice houses occupied by the British. Other than the Government House and the British Council there was less British influence than I expected. We stayed at a nice hotel. Pat and I had a big, lovely, air-conditioned room with good beds which we could not resist, so we got plenty of sleep, as there was nothing else to do. We did manage a game of tennis on the British Club private court.

On Sunday night a British Council movie was shown at the hotel. The Big Event of the week. Like royalty, the British Governor and his entourage, dressed in white dinner jackets, and their ladies in printed cotton frocks, filed into the reserved seats on the front rows. Looking very elegant they seemed out of place in the large barren room with a few rows of folding metal chairs arranged in front of a makeshift cloth screen. Before leaving this morning we shopped in the only British store, not unlike a 1930's country store in small-town America. We bought a few things we can't get here, like Johnson's baby oil, breakfast cereals and English cigarettes.

I dread returning to work tomorrow. Getting back on the treadmill is difficult after the freedom of a holiday. But I must say it's nice to be back in my comfortable house and to know that by tomorrow night all my dirty, red-dust-covered clothes will be clean again without any effort on my part.

(Saturday 18 March)

I'm still groggy and weak from a sudden mysterious illness. I worked until after midnight on Tuesday. Wednesday morning I went to the office feeling a bit rocky and thought it was fatigue. I was working right along when suddenly I started crying. I was just as surprised as my boss, who immediately looked at my eyes to see if they were yellow (we live in fear of hepatitis).

About an hour later I started getting chills. The office thermometer registered my temp as 100 degrees. By this time my boss had gone out. I continued working, keeping the thermometer in my mouth. When it reached 101 I locked away my half-encoded message, left a note for my boss and drove myself home.

By the time I got in bed my teeth were chattering. Mamadou brought out all my blankets and piled them on top of me. Then standing at the foot of my bed he said, *"Mademoiselle ne pleurez pas"* Don't cry. I always cry when I have to give in to illness. I feel so humiliated and helpless. When my fever reached 102 I called my boss to get a doctor. I was having terrible pains in my back and stomach.

By five o'clock when a French doctor arrived my temperature hadn't gone down. Very casually he examined me, mumbled something about malaria and wrote out a prescription for pills. "If your temperature is not back to normal by morning, call me," he said as he left.

I was a bit delirious so American Pat stayed with me through the night. Nausea and stomach pains made me so weak I couldn't hold my head up. My 102-degree fever didn't break until the next morning. Even now, two days later, I still don't have an appetite and find it difficult to sit up, but I must make an effort, otherwise I will get depressed. I've had lots of guests, who brought flowers and good cheer. My boss comes every day.

(Wednesday 22 March)

No wonder I wasn't getting any better! Yesterday my boss was at my bedside when Mamadou brought my pills. Curious, my boss checked the bottles and dosage. He discovered that Mamadou was giving me an overdose of the very medicine that Headquarters had warned employees in Africa to stop taking. Thank goodness he was there and checked out the medicine, otherwise I might have never got well.

Tomorrow is the end of Ramadan. Mamadou had been so good to look after me I gave him some money and the afternoon off.

(Next Day)

I feel suspended in space and time. I can't just relax and take advantage of my illness to lie in bed and read. That strong, nagging sense of duty (my greatest cross to bear) to answer friend's letters, catch up on my work at the office, study French. Time has been my worst enemy since I was a child

(Two days later)

Yesterday I had just come out of a deep, feverish sleep. My room was dark, the outside shutters had been closed for days. Through cracks I could see sunlight and bits of swaying trees. I imagined that a blue sky reflected the sea, which I could hear beating against the cliffs in the dark, silent morning hours. Were the bougainvillea and hibiscus still at the height of their purple and red shades? And the hard green limes, on the tree's spindly limbs, must be ripe by now. I could almost taste their acid freshness, soon to be served to me with sweet, white flesh of fish bought up from the sea by natives whose life depended on the nourishment of this underwater treasure.

Inside my high-ceilinged room a gentle breeze, through the open window, brought a faint sound of street noise mingled with the rustle of leaves. Through the open bedroom door I could see the shadow patterns of the trees on the living room's pale gray walls.

I lay silently, thinking and not wanting to think. I shivered, not from fever which has gripped my body in its burning hands and left my mind powerless to function, but to the awakening of reality of the nothingness in my life. I looked back to the beginning of my long journey of adventure. Pearl Harbor had been bombed, my boyfriend volunteered for the Army and I went to work for the War Department in Washington, D.C . . .

I was just about to grasp the long twisted thread that would eventually bring me through the years from Japan, to Turkey, Iran, Pakistan, India, and Europe when I heard a familiar French-accented voice.

"Elizabet!"

The ghosts of the past quickly faded as I raised my head from the damp pillow and watched Jacqueline, in a red knit dress, her shiny black hair catching bits of sunlight as she tiptoed across the hallway to my bedroom.

"*Comment allez vous?*" She was at my bedside holding out her hand.

"Much better. The fever has subsided. The doctor says I can return to work next week."

She brought a chair to my bedside and eased down as though afraid of disturbing me. I noticed dark circles under her eyes and lines of nervous strain around her mouth. I wondered if her husband had abused her.

I was about to ask what decisions she'd made about her marriage, when a siren wailed right outside my front gate.

She stiffened and turned pale. I could see fear in her eyes.

"What's wrong?" I reached out and took her hand.

For a moment she didn't speak as if she hadn't heard me. Then as though coming out of a spell, she said, "It's the war. I still freeze with fear every time I hear a siren."

"Tell me about your experiences," I urged, not feeling well enough for a lengthy French conversation.

"I was only ten when the war started," she paused and a faint smile touched her lips, "I thought it was all great fun, as we piled our precious belongings into our family car, until mother, who was to drive us to safety in the countryside, told me I couldn't take all my toys. I cried a bit, but soon forgot as we moved slowly in a convoy along the road leading out of my village in Normandy. I was especially thrilled when I saw my cousin, who seemed hardly older than me, driving her father's car. She seemed so grown up.

"We stayed in a pine forest near the sea along the west coast of France. I felt real freedom for the first time in my life, as I ran among the tall trees making belief that I was a fairy with a magic wand that could turn the trees into playmates at any time I wished. Our lodgings were uncomfortable and the facilities were a bit crude, but I was happy in my own forest where at the bottom of almost every tree was a little pot, placed, I thought for my own use. So each morning I used to find a new one, always pleased with such a wide choice. One day I heard my mother complaining of the toilet facilities and I told her of my wonderful discovery. She scolded me and told me that the pots had not been put there for my use, but to catch the resin from the trees."

Jackie's expressions in English provoked images of her peeing in the pots. We laughed so long and loud that Mamadou came to see if anything was wrong. When the laughter faded Jackie looked serious again, as though caught in the memory of a tragic side of her experience. Afraid that she wouldn't continue, I asked quickly, "What about your father, where was he?"

She smiled again as she told me how happy they were after they returned home after realizing there was no use going further south. Soon her father joined them. He had been ill and released from the army. Then there were the lean years of black bread and dried beans in vinegar, but there were amusing incidents, moments of feeling grown up when she had to wear her mother's cast off shoes because there were no more to fit her. She remembered the feasts they had after her father rode his bicycle into the countryside and gathered fresh eggs and vegetables. One anecdote followed another and her colorful English brought sudden snatches of laughter floating around the darkened room.

Then all at once Jackie's face turned dark again as she recounted the last terrifying days of being bombed by the allied forces. She switched to French and the words rushed out, tumbling over one another.

"The allied planes kept coming," she was saying. "The pudding my mother had baked from the last bits of our provisions, and the cool bottles of wine, the last from our cellar, waiting to be served to our liberators, were covered in dust and fallen bits of plaster. Our best linen table cloth for the occasion was hidden in the debris that kept falling from the ceiling as the bombs hit, one after the other and in groups of explosions like a dynamite factory on fire.

"We were in shock of disbelief. We sat around the table we had prepared to share with our American liberators, unable to move. Then like scared rabbits we hid in the stairwell. The bombs kept falling, znnnnnnnn BOOOOOOOMMMM." She was waving her arms and her eyes were wide in the terror of remembering.

"The house shook, and wavered back and forth. I wanted to scream and run, but my father kept holding me back. We stayed there for hours, cramped and terrified and bewildered. The bombs kept coming, znnnnnn BOOOMMMMMM. I will never forget the sound and even now I shake with fright when I hear a formation of planes in the sky. Finally my father said that there was no use staying on. We might be able to escape. We ran from the house stopping only to grab our bicycles. I gave mine to our maid and rode with my father. We were soon caught up in the crowd of screaming people, unable, like ourselves to believe that the bombs were falling from allied planes. The Germans were fleeing to surrounding countryside. We were all running together. I lost my shoes because they were my mothers and too big to run in. We slept in a meadow for two days. We sat in the cellar of an old Normandy farm house for another eternity. Fright had been replaced by fatigue. And then we found a small abandoned house on a farm." She paused and caught her breath. "We lay down on the beds, not caring anymore. The city burned in the distance, but there was fresh milk and real butter, and it was summer and I didn't mind being barefooted. But one morning we were awakened by the sound of a heavy boot on the door. My father opened it and I could see, in the early morning light, dozens of Germans running to and fro and under each apple tree there was a tank. The German, who had kicked the door was telling my father that we had better move on if we didn't want to be killed by our own allies. Although he said this in a sarcastic tone, he was kind all the same. We were allowed to use the roadway, although warned that it was dangerous. We crossed bridges, guarded by stern, but sympathetic Germans with machine guns. Then the strafing began. We tumbled into ditches. I could see the dust from the road rising in lines as bullets bounced like hailstones. They were coming closer. Someone grabbed me and dragged me deeper into the hedge. When it was all over I looked up into the face of a Germany soldier. He smiled and asked me, in broken French, if I was all right. For a moment he looked at me, as a father might look as his own child, and said, 'I have daughter like you.'" She paused. "I will never forget the tears in his eyes."

As though this memory had brought some tender relief, her voice trailed off and her eyes looked a bit dazed.

An uncomfortable silence followed. I felt ashamed that I had encouraged her to relive an emotional memory, which she had told with such childish emotion that she now seemed self—conscious and embarrassed.

Then without warning she began to laugh. "I came to cheer you up and we are both in tears and it's already lunch time."

After she left, I was just about the take an aspirin for my tense headache, brought on by all that emotion, when I heard my name being called from the doorway. This time it was with a German accent, and there stood Hilda (the wife of a colleague), smiling down at me. Her blond hair, bleached by the sun, looked almost white against her tanned, square face. Her blue eyes always seemed guarded as though they defended secrets.

"I've come to bring you some strudel." She handed it to Mamadou, who had followed her into the room to see if we would like coffee. She said that she had just finished lunch and I suggested Mamadou bring iced limeade instead.

I looked at her face and wondered what had caused the deep creases on her forehead. All of a sudden I had to know how she fared during the war.

"Hilda," I asked, "where were you during the war?"

Her face showed momentary surprise by the question, but for a moment she didn't react. She was more poised and self—possessed than Jackie. But I saw the tiny muscles in her face tighten.

"Berlin. Why do you ask?" Her voice was controlled.

"Because the war had a great influence on my life, and yet I know so little about it from the viewpoint of those who experienced it." I could see that she didn't really want to talk about World War II, but somehow I felt she would not mind if she knew that I was a sympathetic listener.

Before I could get her started talking Mamadou came in with a tray of cold limeade and cookies.

The tart refreshing liquid soothed my dry throat. I waited until she had sipped her drink and then asked, "Did you stay in Berlin all the time?"

Slowly at the beginning, then in gushes her story came out.

She was thirteen when the war started. Her mother had died some years before. She lived with her father in a big farm house, outside Berlin, and helped him by overseeing the feeding of the farm workers. Soon after the war began her father had to join the army. She was left alone to manage with the help of an old man who had been with them for as many years as she could remember. Later on, French prisoners were sent to help on the farm. She was too young to understand war, but she was not too young to understand the meaning of "prisoner." She secretly shared her food with the prisoners and would sneak them bits of her father's clothing when the weather was cold. And then the bombing of Berlin began. Her father had told her to run to the bottom of the garden where there were double walls with space between them for her to crouch.

She never became accustomed to the bombings and always ran out to watch the planes in the distance. One day as she stood watching them, one broke formation and headed for her house. She ran to the double wall and fell on her face on the cool damp ground. She heard the noise of the bomb and then the next thing she remembered was something cold and wet on her face. She opened her eyes and stared into those of a French prisoner she had befriended. He was washing her face. The tender way he looked at her she imagined that he must be thinking of his own children. When the bomb hit she was buried in the debris, but luckily the prisoners knew where to look for her and had dug her out before she suffocated. The bomb damaged the house and killed the old man who had helped on the farm. From then on the French prisoners protected her.

When the war ended word came that her father had been killed. She clung to the French prisoner who had saved her life, terrified to be left alone and helpless.

Hilda had told the last bit of her story with such unexpected emotion that I couldn't bear for her to go on, so I changed the subject. Later, when she regained control of her emotions, she told me that the Frenchman stayed with her until a distant relative could take over the farm.

(Wednesday 29 March)

I was in bed only ten days. The doctor asked what was my secret to such quick recovery. A strong will power, I told him.

This morning I'm suffering a rare hangover. Two American Navy ship were in harbor and I was drafted to "dance with the officers." I didn't want to go, but my boss, who is getting concerned about my life being all work and no play, almost ordered me to go.

I had already met the officers at a dance given by the Ambassador when they were here last month. Since then they have been cruising around the Atlantic, chasing the Portuguese ship *Santa Maria*, hijacked on 22 January in West Indian waters by an armed band of Portuguese political insurgents. The hijackers, led by Captain Henrique Galvao, were protesting the Iberian dictators, Franco in Spain and Salazar in Portugal. They planned to take over the island of Fernando Po and later Portuguese Angola.

The U.S. ship caught up with the *Santa Maria* and Admiral Smith, negotiated with Captain Galvao and made arrangements for him to give up the *Santa Maria*.

The commodore told me, at the dance, that Galvao was a very kind, humanitarian, an intellectual and not the sort of man who would hijack a ship. But he agreed that Galvao's aim to call world attention to the Dictators certainly worked. I got home at 3:30 this morning.

(Thursday 30 March)

Last night I went to a *Misshui* (North African dish made with roast lamb) party given by an Embassy officer. We gathered in his back garden and had drinks around a big bonfire over which two lambs roasted. When they were done, we ate chunks of tender meat smothered in hot sauce. For dessert ice cream, topped with hot fudge, was a great treat. Then we saw his movies of East African game parks. Extremely enjoyable evening.

(Saturday 1 April)

Senegal will celebrate its independence, beginning Monday. The country has spent millions of francs getting ready. Buildings painted, flags hung (some from eleven-story buildings) main streets repaired (the back ones are still full of potholes and lined with garbage) villas redecorated to house delegates. To add to the few hotel rooms available, a ship has been hired from France, fully staffed with French chefs, waiters, etc. Nothing has been spared to put up a good facade. It's ridiculous for such a poor country, but a necessity these days for the pride and self-esteem of underdeveloped countries. Each must try to outdo the other.

The U.S. is honoring the event by sending vice-president Johnson to attend the festivities, which means a lot of work for the Embassy. I've hardly seen my boss. He was delegated to assist the secret service men who have been here for four days. The Ambassador is giving a reception for Johnson next Tuesday to which all Embassy staff are invited. We have a four-day holiday, beginning this morning, but I will be on duty and can't count on even one full day of my own.

(Monday 3 April)

I didn't even get Sunday off. I did go to the beach in the morning, but was at my desk in the Embassy by three o'clock and emerged at nine practically blind and with writer's cramp from doing code work. I had to call off dinner with British friends and meet them later at the big square in front of the embassy for the Torchlight Parade.

It was a beautiful warm night with a full moon. When the parade finally arrived, an hour late, everything was mass confusion. The President's guard, tall, black men dressed in bright-red uniforms, arrived on horseback carrying flaming torches. Then came hundreds of men dressed in yellow robes, also carrying torches. Hordes of people crowded the square. Little children rushed around throwing fire crackers.

Dakar was swarming with tribes from the bush. Their faces and bodies colorfully painted, in various patterns, they brought their own dancers and drummers. There was even a group from Mauritania dancing to their strange music, waving shotguns in the air and shooting blank bullets at one another. The Falups came with their spears and bows and arrows. Their black shiny bodies danced, and danced, and danced in the torchlight. The Mauritania's whirled and leaped with their shotguns raised high in the air. The celebration veered out of control. The police disbursed the swarming crowds with flaming torches (Imagine!) and I was caught in the stampede. The only unanimated participants were the torch bearers, pathetic looking as they trudged along in their homemade costumes of yellow cotton baggy trousers, brief tops, and knitted wool caps to match. Their faces completely blank, they halfheartedly held up their torches, some of which had long ago burned out, they straggled along, bringing up the rear.

I was sure I could buy movie film here. Wrong! So I had to watch the most exciting African spectacle I will ever see and was unable to record it.

There will be more parades and tonight I hope to see some African dancing in the moonlight to the music of the tom-toms. The Africans are good dancers, even little girls. They dance by themselves in a circle, around the drums. The women dance in one circle and the men in another. This is the way they express their feelings, or please the gods when they want rain, or frighten off evil spirits. Jitterbug is a form of African dance.

(Yesterday—Sunday 2 April)

The Ambassador gave a reception to meet Vice President Johnson and Lady Bird. They shook hands warmly with us and both gave speeches, telling us how important our work was (!), and how glad they were that the natives really "liked" them (!). This American mania for wanting to be "liked" I find distasteful. If we care about what people "think" then we should be concerned about respect. By wanting to be liked we put ourselves at risk of blackmail by two-bit foreign politicians seeking power, i.e. "Either you give us aid or we won't like you." And we fall for it. The greatest power in the world groveling at the feet of third world governments because they want to be liked. How undignified! But then dignity is something our politicians are not strong on. Imagine standing along the roadway with thousands of Africans while watching the cortege of cars, carrying representatives of all countries, filing past in their dignified manner. Then comes the big American car, flying the U.S.A. flag on one fender and the Embassy flag on the other, out of which hangs a great hulk of a man with a Madison Avenue grin, his hands clasped like a victorious prize fighter, waving to the people as if to say "I'm the greatest!" And then later to give out pencils like a traveling salesman.

The Peace Corps sent a young, unsophisticated Baptist minister, who didn't speak French to sum up the situation. (AUTHOR'S NOTE: This was Bill Moyers, whom I misjudged because of his naiveté at that time. He is now one of the few men I admire.) The V-P introduced him as a Peace Corps leader and said that Moyers was making a great sacrifice by giving up his high-paying job to work for nothing to help save the world. If one makes sacrifices at least it should not be thrown in the faces of those for whom they are made, especially if the sacrifice wasn't wanted. Senegal, not having asked for Peace Corps workers, was angry when the *Herald Tribune* Paris edition printed a long article about the findings of Peace Corps representative (Moyer), "who visited a village on the outskirts of Dakar for a couple of hours while the V-P was being photographed giving out pencils to the natives." And it must be remembered, the article continued, the representative could speak neither the local language nor French. The American had found, according to the article, filth, flies, disease, lack of food and sanitary conditions with which the poor sacrificing Peace Corps workers would have to contend. It went on to say how it would be necessary to send out a doctor with each group and Peace Corps workers would have to come into Dakar periodically to have a proper bath.

This went down like a lead balloon . . . especially since Senegal has not even asked for Peace Corps workers. Really how much longer are we going to be so ignorant of foreign cultures. If we can't stay at home and mind our own business, at least we might learn good manners. I heard that V-P Johnson called the hairdresser and demanded that she come in on Sunday and fix his secretary's hair. This sort of thing doesn't "work" with French Colons, who have the French attitude that they are culturally superior to the Americans.

(Thursday 5 April)

The Ambassador closed the Embassy today because we had worked so hard for the V-P's visit. The Ambassador's secretary and I took advantage of the deserted golf course and had a nice 18-hole game. It is a pretty sad course. Adjoining the beach, at least it has grassy greens and the sea breeze. I would like to join the Golf Club, but I can afford only one club and I prefer the Riding Club.

(Sunday 9 April)

I'm exhausted. I gave a big dinner party last night. Fourteen guests. Six Africans, four Brits from the British Embassy, one Frenchman who dances a mean cha-cha-cha, my boss and his wife. It was my first try at mixing groups and languages. I think it turned out all right but I wasn't too pleased. A good party needs a hard core of friends who come to help entertain and not just sit and be entertained. Also I needed a man to act as host. Some of the guests didn't speak English. I was so harassed with a poorly organized kitchen that I found it difficult to concentrate sufficiently to be a good hostess in a foreign language.

(Monday 10 April)

Mamadou's neat appearance always puzzled me. How could he clean the house, do laundry and cook, wash dishes, and always look so neat in his starched white tunic over royal-blue Arabian-nights trousers? Today I found out.

About midmorning I rushed home to pick up some papers from my desk and found Mamadou busily scrubbing the floors. Clad only in a pair of very, very short French shorts he looked so naked and defenseless. Without his flowing robes, he was as ordinary-looking as a porter in the bazaar. Regretting my intrusion, which embarrassed both of us and spoiled my African-King image of him, I left without the papers I had come for.

(Saturday 15 April)

This has been a hectic week. I haven't been in bed before one-thirty since last Thursday night a week ago. Four nights I worked until 0130 hours. The other nights I either went out to dinner or to the movies, which begin at 9:15 p.m. and end about one in the morning. My boss finally got off yesterday on a two-week vacation. First he had to go to Paris on business, then on to

Spain where his wife will join him. I will stay with their four children.

LATER..What happened to the day? Answer: Worked all morning. Had big lunch (Hors d'oeuvres of Potato, onions, eggs, tomato etc.; fish soufflé, fresh lettuce salad, cheese, butter and French bread, fresh pineapple, coffee and a half-bottle of good red wine.) Mamadou is such a good cook I've heard that the Ambassador's wife has her eye on him.

Bought a new cha-cha-cha record, my birthday present to myself, which cost $5.00! In the States it would cost no more than two or three dollars. Fetched Amy, my French teacher, had a lesson and returned her home. A phone call from American Pat made me late for a cocktail party at the University. On the way I stopped by to pick up an American couple and found that the husband had gone on and left her in bed, threatened by a miscarriage. So I stayed with her until he returned. It was midnight before I got home.

(Sunday 16 April) My Birthday!

Woke up at 7:30 to a lovely room filled with cool shadows, bright sunlight filtering through the shutters and a soft sea breeze. I was very comfortable and almost happy until I realized it was my birthday..my 38th! I felt a deep pain of loneliness, but rather than wallow in the slime of self-pity I promised myself that all would be changed by next 16th of April, for better or for worse. All these years I have comforted myself with the idealistic thought that if I remain calm, do my duty toward life, get as much out of every moment as possible, eventually I would find the pot of gold at the end of the rainbow. Now I know better. The 'pot of gold' is a thousand precious moments, like jewels, scattered throughout one's life, to be gathered along the way. Up to now I have gathered my share, but I've come to a crossroad. I must decide which way I will go.

(Wednesday 19 April)

I have made a decision. I've had enough of 'all work and no play'. Dakar is the last straw. I am going to ask for a year's leave of absence. If not granted I hope I have the courage to resign. Before the last flame of youth, already flickering, dies, I am going to have myself a fling. No definite plans, but winter on the European ski slopes should get the old blood circulating again. I'm fed up with underdeveloped countries and cultural vacuums. What I need is a bit of overdevelopment in a cold climate. If I find my blood is too thin I can always return to India and live with my friend Maya and her family. When I was in bed with malaria I had a wonderful dream of a little house perched high on a cliff, overlooking the Mediterranean, complete with a vineyard and a lover. Too much of Durell's *Bitter Lemons?*

(Thursday 20 April)

Little time for my diary since my boss and his wife left for Spain. In addition to running the office single handed I have taken over guardianship of my bosses children (ages 9, 7, 4 and 1) and will stay with them in their apartment. This morning With the help of the nanny I finally got the three oldest ones off to the beach with their playmates' mother. After lunch I took the one-year-old to my house and settled him in his basket in the garden while I cut back the bougainvillea. Everything was going along well until I turned on the hose, which frightened the baby. He started crying and it took me an hour to quieten him. There went my chance to hang the pictures, which have been lined up against the wall for weeks.

I'm getting a bit panicky. My house guest, Josephine, will arrive by tramp steamer from New York and I haven't even got a bed for my spare room. Having to supervise the boss' servants and do all the office work, I have to run at high speed from 0600 to midnight. And this morning I found my car had a flat tire! Woe is me.

(Wednesday 26 April)

My daily routine while staying overnight at my boss's house: Out of bed at six o'clock, take up the one-year-old baby, change his diaper, wash his hands and face and feed him a bowl of something that looks like starch. Meanwhile the nanny has got the other three children dressed and to the table. I have breakfast with them, get the two oldest boys off to school and then turn my attention to taking four-year-old Ann to kindergarten, located between her house and mine. I hurry on to my house, rush to the kitchen, make coffee and while drinking it, with my morning cigarette, I try to write a few lines. I'm always late for work, but after I get the children into bed at night I return to the office and work until midnight.

Josephine's arrival has been delayed. Meanwhile I've got another house guest. The secretary of our Ambassador in Conakry (Guinea) arrived yesterday to have work done on her teeth. There were no hotel rooms available. I offered my bed. Pictures will never be hung, but I'm glad to do something for her. Life in Conakry is very difficult. Guinea is practically an iron curtain country and the people are very anti-American. When they got their independence they threw out all the French and now there is not one decent doctor or dentist in the country.

(Thursday 27 April)

What a hectic day. Late yesterday afternoon I (the only CIA representative in the embassy) was presented to four very high-ranking Foreign Service Officers, on a trip around Africa (the latest "in" continent), as part of a Senior Foreign Policy course they've just completed in Washington. When I asked what I could do for them they said they wanted to meet some non-official

Africans and had been told that I was the only one in the Embassy who had a circle of local friends. I explained that my friends were young University students. Perfect! they said. With that I invited them to lunch the following day.

After work I rushed home. Simply had to plant some flower seedlings I'd bought days ago and were now almost dead. So when I picked up my French teacher, Amy, I took her on a wild goose chase buying gardening implements. She removed her shoes and helped me dig holes and cover the plants. This finished, we were getting down to French grammar when I remembered the luncheon party. This took up the rest of our time with still no assurance that she could contact all the students on my list and get them to my house by noon the next day.

(Next day, Friday 28 April)

When Mamadou arrived at seven thirty I announced that there would be twelve for lunch, his eyes widened and he opened his mouth, but kept quiet. I took the morning off to help him buy the food. After three hours at the market we started getting the house ready. My guest pitched in. I borrowed card tables and we set them up in the living room. We made my study into a bar, where we had drinks (African friends, Moslems, don't drink alcohol) before sitting down to lunch. After *hors d'oeuvres* Mamadou served a four-course meal with lots of wine for the Americans and soft drinks for the Africans. It was 3:30 when we finished a successful lunch, all conducted in French, except my English translations for the Marine Colonel, who didn't speak French.

This luncheon might not have happened had we had an accredited Ambassador, who could have presented the VIPs to the Senegalese Government officials. But the Senegalese Government has not announced the new American Ambassador. The VIPs wanted to meet Africans, naturally, and since they couldn't meet government officials, they made do with University students Frankly, they probably found out more about the

Senegalese attitude toward America from these students. It has been my experience that government officials are not always forth—coming about their true feelings about a country. That's called diplomacy. But students don't have any such restrictions. In any case the VIPs seemed pleased with their meeting.

The outgoing Ambassador came to tell me good-bye. I sensed he hadn't expected his recall. He seemed distraught. He told me that I was his favorite person in the Embassy. I was surprised. It's true he has invited me to diplomatic receptions, but only, so I thought, because I speak a little French.

(Sunday 30 April)

Visiting VIPs left yesterday (Saturday) morning and I worked all afternoon until time to go to the Ambassador's residence to bid "bon voyage". We are sorry to see him go. He was well liked by everyone.

After the reception I went to an African Diplomatic party. The only other white guests were two Frenchmen. Interesting to see the customs and behavior of young Africans, who represent their country abroad as I do mine. Among themselves they shed some of their Western refinement and manners and are more natural and unselfconscious. At one point I found a couple of men in the kitchen eating out of a pot on the stove. It is a compliment to be trusted and accepted by them. They are excellent dancers and I regretted leaving the party at 0300 hours while they were still cha-cha-chaing.

I got up at seven this morning to have breakfast with the boss' children and get them off to church. While the maid took them to mass I came home and got dressed in time to see the Ambassador off on a ship bound for France. Before lunch I took the children to a church fair and after lunch we went to the airport to welcome their parents.

Soon after we arrived back at their apartment the presents were distributed (I got a lovely gold bracelet, a bottle each of sherry and port wine from Spain and a book of drawings). I brought my boss up to date on what had happened at the office and then came home. It is now only five o'clock, but I'm going to bed.

(Monday 1 May)

Received a beautiful carved Balinese head from and admirer with whom I served in Tehran. He is now in the American Embassy in Djakarta. Pity I couldn't fall in love with him. He is really a fine person, but not mysterious enough for me.

(Tuesday 2 May)

My house guest, Josephine, arrived today by freighter from New York and will stay until 22 May. She retired at sixty (with a good income) and looks fifteen years younger. Her eyes no longer look tired and the dark circles have disappeared. Her mousy hair looks thicker and healthier. She smiles and laughs easier and her clothes are more modern and brighter colors.

She doesn't agree with my plans to stop working for a year, but I explained that I had rather work when I'm too old to ski and after I satisfy, somewhat, my spirit of adventure.

(Wednesday 17 May)

Fifteen days have passed. No way can I write in detail about what Josephine and I have done. But I'll make a list, otherwise blank spaces in my diary will indicate I missed many days of my life. I gave a dinner party for Jo, as she's called, on the 5th of May to introduce her to my British, French and American friends. We went to African dance program on the sixth and witnessed the frenzied killing of a sacrificial chicken on the stage. Jo was always so formal in the office, I was happily surprised that she enjoyed the dances and didn't mind being one of two white faces in the audience. Also, it was her idea to go to Varela. She is certainly a more adventurous since she retired.

On the seventh (Sunday) we left for Varela, Portuguese Guinea (where Magda and I went), but this time it wasn't much fun. The bush had dried up, it was hot and dusty and we saw few people along the way. Driving across two logs over a black-water hole in the jungle still made my heart race with fear. We had a lovely cottage in Varela, two bedrooms and a bath, in the pine forest, overlooking the Atlantic. The water was warm for swimming and the nights cool for sleeping. Our first morning on the beach I left Jo lying on the powder-white sand while I took a long walk on the deserted beach. Being alone I went native and removed my bikini top as I walked a mile or so on a band of dazzling sand between the cobalt-blue Atlantic and the vibrant green jungle.

On the way back, ahead of me, a tribesman in a scanty loin cloth, carrying a bow and arrow, stepped out of the dense, dark jungle and turned down the beach toward Jo. She was lying on her stomach, obviously unaware of his presence. I put on my bikini top and started walking faster and faster, concerned about what might happen. I suppressed my urge to run for fear of frightening him. As his shadow fell across Jo I was afraid she might scream and excite him, but she casually turned over and looked up at him. By this time I was close enough to call out softly to her, "Don't pick up your camera." At the sound of my voice he jerked around and raised his bow. I quickly bowed as I'd seen them do to one another. (A courtly gesture picked up from the Portuguese?) We smiled at him and he backed away, turned and disappeared into the dense bush.

(Our last Day in Varela)

Last night I fell asleep reading *Lafcadio's Adventures* by Andre Gide and after a restless night, on a hard, knotty bed, awakened at dawn. While Jo slept, I went to the beach.

The sea was calm. I went for a swim and a long walk, bare to the hips, in the warm early-morning sun.

Now I'm back at the cottage with my diary before me. Through the open window I can see two Falup tribesmen, bows and arrows swinging from their sides, moving through patches of sunlight in the forest below my window. These past two days, in 'another world', have transformed me. I dread the long, hot, eleven-hour drive back to reality.

(Saturday 20 May)

How glad I'll be when this day ends. Before I went to Varela I invited fifty people (a mixture of British, American, Portuguese, French and Africans) to a costume party tonight. I expect them to arrive this evening at 9:30 p.m. in fancy dress, dance until midnight, eat their supper and go home sometime before dawn.

Meanwhile Jo and I will spend the day supervising the house cleaning and cooking. I have hired three extra servants to help Mamadou. The front garden will be turned into a sort of cafe with tables and chairs. Two hired African musicians will strum on their *kora* and *balafone*. The living room and my study will be the dance halls and the back garden, the bar. I will serve cold meat (ham, beef and lamb), corn, three salads, French bread, butter and wine and fruit salad and coffee for desert. All with plenty of both white and red wine. A professional photographer will record the event. I've told Mamadou that I want to enjoy my party and not have to supervise.

(Next day)

The party got started on a bad note. I emerged from my bedroom as the Queen of Outer Space: black long—sleeved, high-necked tights, black ballet slippers, a long red satin cape trimmed in silver, and a splendid Balinese-type silver helmet. I had powdered my face white, darkened around my eyes, wore blood-red lipstick and carried a silver wand.

On the way to receive my guests I checked the bar. There were no highball glasses. I was furious.

I stormed to the kitchen. Threw open the door. Mamadou was sitting on the floor, with his back to me, opening raw oysters. "Mamadou!" I yelled, "where are the glasses for the bar?" He doesn't like to be bossed by a woman, especially in the presence of his peers (naturally) so he was slow to look over his shoulder. When he saw me he almost went white. I had been transformed from the ordinary mistress of the house into some sort of an evil spirit. He stared at me and the expression of disbelief seemed to freeze on his face.

One of the other servants picked up a tray of glasses and I turned and joined the first guests. From then on Mamadou couldn't keep his eyes off me. I would catch him peering at me from behind a tree in the dimly-lit garden, or through a crack in the kitchen door. He was worthless for the rest of the night. (I understood his reactions better the following day when I put myself in his position and realized that maybe he thought I had some magic powers. After all that same costume won first place as "That Old Black Magic" in a come-as-a-song—title costume party in India.)

Everyone came in fancy dress. Africans wore costumes representing West-African countries. Jo looked good in my best Indian sari and a red dot on her forehead. The party began in the back garden with drinks and *hors d'oeuvres*. After everyone had arrived and with drinks in hand we moved to the front garden to hear the African musicians. Dressed in white they sat regally on a red Persian carpet, under a lime tree in the middle of the garden, and played their droning music.

After the concert we went inside and paraded in a circle around the living room so judges could choose the best costumes. Native African costumes of the last century won as best couple. The best gentleman's costume was our handsome young diplomat, dressed as Nero in a white toga and a garland of green ferns around his head. The best lady's costume was a young woman from the West Indies in her native costume.

The other servants watched the parade, but Mamadou stood in the dim background, surreptitiously watching me.

After dancing, supper was served, and the last guest left about three o'clock. According to the servants, Mamadou went home right after supper, "*mal de tête*," with a headache. This morning, when he came to work, he would not look me in the eye and all through the day I felt him staring at me, then quickly averting his eyes when I looked his way.

(Monday 22 May)

Jo has just left on a plane to Casablanca and I find the house empty and lonely. I am weary and restless. I even feel cut off from my work. Today is a holiday. I have not been to the office in three days. I should go to work tonight, but I can't face it. I'm so far behind I'll have work every night this week.

Having Jo here gave me a look into the future. She has done her duty, served her country for forty years and now she is free **at sixty years old** to travel. Her best years spent in a career she didn't want either. At the end of her visit she could see I was desperate. She realized what working in this frame of mind does to me. Makes me a monster. And I don't want to be one. She finally agreed that I was making a wise decision to quit while I could still enjoy life.

(Tuesday 23 May)

Yesterday before I could get dressed to receive my Portuguese friend, Luis, and his wife, Milu, who has just arrived from Portugal, the garden gate bell rang. I thought it might be them arriving early, but when I opened the gate there stood the musicians of the night before, still wearing their magnificent white robes. One had brought his shy wife, dressed in an elaborate pink cotton boubou and turban to match. The bulky robe over her short body made her look like a big blob of cotton candy with a black, round, smiling face and a glint of gold in her teeth.

I invited them in and after many exaggerated compliments,

on both sides, the negotiating for their services began. It's hard to bargain with them. They always say, "Give me what you think my services were worth." (Perhaps thinking that you will give them more than they dare ask for.) You reply, "It's better you tell me your price (hoping it will be less than you would have offered). This goes on for a few minutes and finally the price is named. In my case it was 10,000 Francs (about $40.00). I was shocked and furious at myself for not setting the price before I hired them. Fortunately I had only 7,500 Francs in my handbag for which they settled. (Note: Later my African friends told me that I paid three times what the cost should have been, but I'm glad they made a little extra.)

After I paid them I hoped they would go so I could change my dress and comb my hair, but no, they didn't budge from my sofa where they all three sat in full formal dress (white khaftan and red fez for men) smiling from ear to ear with glints of gold in their gleaming white teeth. Since we didn't understand one another's French, the long silences were interspersed with nervous outbursts of laughter.

Finally when Luis and Milu arrived they looked a bit surprised at the scene, not knowing if my guests were friends. Mamadou, who still peers at me out of the corner of his eye, said something to the musicians, or they might have stayed for dinner.

Luis has been here a couple of months and we have become good friends. He is about my age, medium height, thin with a pale face and big dark eyes behind thick glasses. He is not handsome but is charming, with "old world" manners, and intelligent. He speaks impeccable French and English and has been a great help, acting as host, during my Sunday evening salons when all my French friends gather for discussions on art and literature. They seemingly were never aware that I rarely understood what they are saying. I just laugh with them and when they look serious I follow suite.

I wasn't expecting Milu to be so pretty and smart. She is petite, with a pixie face and a short Italian hair cut. She also speaks perfect French, but no English, and will be an addition to my dinner parties. She's just as talkative and warm as he is.

(Saturday Night 27 May)

After I invited the University English Club to come this afternoon for a square dancing lesson (what a farce, I have no idea how to square dance. I make it up as I go along), I realized that my record player, damaged during my last big party, was in the repair shop. I couldn't face trying to borrow one so I asked Amy to contact the students and postpone the lesson.Most of them didn't get the message and showed up. I gave them tea and cake and took them to a movie. Luckily there was a good one showing. I have finally received *Clea*, the last book in Durrell's quartet, and I'm dying to finish it.

(Sunday 28 May)

After reading in bed all day I finished *Clea*. I closed the book feeling disoriented. The sunset had reached it's height of reds, pinks and golds. I saw everything outside my window as through for the first time. The hibiscus, a shade redder than the sky, poked their frail heads above the window sill. At the end of the garden, taller and darker green bushes and purple bougainvillea formed a verdant wall, behind which ancient trees almost blotted out the sky. Their branches, caressed by the wind, waved gently. In the silence I could hear the gentle slap of the sea as it met the shore.

Inside everything looked familiar. The Degas prints on the wall have hung on my bedroom walls in many countries. The little Indian bronze figurines on the bookcase were on a bookcase in my bedroom in India. The perfume of sunshine clinging to the sheets and the pale yellow blanket, under which I have slept in many countries, is the same. Yes, my things were all familiar. And yet, I couldn't connect.

Clea had absorbed my mind and imagination. I had lived it vicariously and when it finished I had to come face to face with memories of the other three books of Durrel's quartet. I read *Justine* in Paris with Ernst when our happiness was at its height. *Mountolive*, I read in a small chalet in the French Alps where I fled with a broken heart after Ernst left me in Paris. *Balthazar* helped me recover from Malaria here in Dakar. And now I'm sad to have finished the last of the quartet, *Clea*.

(Monday 29 May)

I hesitate to dwell on my forthcoming freedom lest it overshadows the present and blinds me to the small pleasures of the moment; my house and garden (sadly in need of care), the sound of the sea, cool evening breezes, excellent food and silent Sundays. So much to share, but no one with whom to share it. So rich in possibilities, but so lonely in reality. I have been here nine months and I haven't met one soul mate of either sex. Amy, my French teacher, puts me in touch with "Africa" and an Irish girl friend's wit makes me laugh. The two Pats give me variety in the way of seeing the world around me.

(Tuesday 30 May)

Having worked fourteen hours on our last holiday, I decided to take this one off and play golf with a couple of women colleagues. Even on difficult sand fairways I won.

Got home at 1:30 and found a message to come to the office. There went my holiday. No wonder I'm turning into a monster. I could only work three hours because I had to go to the University to help the students prepare for their square dancing performance.

(Thursday 1 June)

Last night I stayed late at the office to talk with my boss

about resigning my job. He doesn't want me to leave. For selfish reasons, he admitted. He dreads the thought of trying to find someone else and admits that women like me are hard to find. He doesn't think it's possible to get a year of leave without pay for me. I also pointed out that I haven't had a raise in seven years. I have had to sit back and watch raises given to 26-year-old men who have worked only a few years and who were already making more money than I was. And they wonder why they can't keep "Good Girls" like me. If I finish my tour of duty my boss said that he would see that I get a raise. I told him I needed a sabbatical more than a raise. He can't understand the need I have for a rest, a chance to replenish myself. I told him I had run dry. I have nothing more to give. I didn't tell him that I didn't believe in our foreign policy on Senegal. As far as I can see, Communism is an American problem. We stand to lose our "way of life", whereas most small, poor African countries, living under repressive regimes and struggling to stay alive, have nothing to lose. Why should we expect them to fear communism as we do?

(Friday 2 June)

Jackie came to lunch. Her problems are growing dull. Her husband can't find work, but does not mind spending her hard-earned money. She, poor thing, puts up with his deception. Love is such a powerful and destructive emotion.

Last night I took a couple of Embassy women to see the square dancing performance at the University English Club's last meeting for the school year. It wasn't exactly American square dancing, but it was lively and they seemed to enjoy it. I was afraid they would decide not to perform the dance because of the present anti-American feeling raging through the University campus.

We are losing our reputation as a democracy because of the racial problem in the U.S. African diplomats at the U.N. and in Washington are being humiliated and insulted at every turn. They can't even get a decent place for their embassies, much less a place to live. If this attitude doesn't change we might find pressure from Africa and the Orient to move the U.N. to another country and break diplomatic ties with the U.S. Trying to explain our government, our way of life, and the psychological problem involved in the race problems is difficult. It takes a mature person (black or white) to remain objective in the face of insults and humiliation. Ten million dollars in aid to Africa will be useless as long as the situation in Alabama and the south exists. One student from the English Club went to America on a scholarship (they usually go to England). He returned the other day, bitter and disillusioned. According to Amy, he gave a talk to the English Club in which he said the insults in the south were not as hard to take as those in Washington, D. C. and the north. Amy said that after he finished she doubted that the American Embassy would ever get any students to go to the U.S. Sad, because a program has been launched to get African students to the U.S., to which I'm opposed. Why give them scholarships to enable them to return and give firsthand accounts of the discrimination? One can be a bit removed from such stories in newspapers, but when it happens to someone you know it hurts. American racists should be aware that the U.N. will someday be made up of more blacks than whites and we'd better be making as many U.N. friends as possible; we might not always be rich and powerful. One could argue that racism is a national problem, but the world is growing too small for national problems to be ignored. Unfortunately, our voting masses do not always understand our position as a world leader.

(Sunday 4 June)

I woke up last night to the sound of rain. For a moment I thought I was back in Japan, where it rains a lot. This morning the sky was gray and everything was wet and green. Yesterday the gardener trimmed back the bougainvillea and cut the little patches of grass. The garden looks lovely, especially from my bed, where I spent the morning reading. I'm on a reading jag. I look forward to Sundays when I can lie in bed and read all day. I'm reading a French novel about Dakar. A very interesting insight into the present day problems between Africans and white Europeans; namely intermarriages. Unfortunately, I had to leave my book and go to lunch with Amy and her three sisters. Their parents were out for the day. I stopped on the way and bought roses. It's a strict French custom to take flowers to the hostess. The African food was good, but unfortunately, like other people in underdeveloped countries, everyone was self-conscious eating in the European manner. In India I learned to eat properly with my right hand so as not to embarrass my less sophisticated friends who didn't use cutlery.

(Monday 12 June)

Yesterday (Sunday) morning after tennis I worked until 1:30 then went to a girlie tea party at three o'clock. At five o'clock I took toys and candy to the son of a French woman, married to an African. Poor little child had been very ill and in hospital. His mother wants to teach me French literature, but somehow I can never find time to get started. I went from their poor little flat to the University, collected Amy and took her to a French movie.

After a big dinner, I was in bed with my book. What a dull life for one who has skied in the Japanese Alps, ridden wild horse over the Anatolian Plateau in Turkey, Dined at the palace of the Shah of Iran. Sat beside Ravi Shankar, on floor cushions, while he played the sitar. Lived in Paris, etc.

(Tuesday 13 June)

Today I wrote to Lena, thanking her for her invitation to spend Christmas with her and family in Bonn. I told her I felt sure that she could make a reservation for me at a ski resort in January. I hope to leave in October, if I resign. And I might have to, which means I'll never get that trip around Africa to the Gold Coast, Dahomey, Nigeria etc.

(Wednesday 14 June)

This morning before I went to work I told Mamadou to clean the recently-flooded storage shed and dry it out. I also reminded him that my Portuguese friends were coming to lunch at one o'clock.

It was after one thirty when I got home. Luis and Milu were already there. Luis came forward and embraced me, as is our custom. I looked over his shoulder, horrified at what I saw behind him. There, spread out on the floor in the sunlight, was a whole array of CIA bugging equipment! It had been hidden away in the storage room and forgotten until Mamadou brought it out to dry in the sun. Luis had had plenty of time to examine it. Now he knows for sure that I work for CIA. Both of us pretended we hadn't seen it. I told my boss and he said it was completely outdated, so no harm done.

(Thursday 15 June)

Amy brought good news. She leaves in August for Scotland where she will assist in the French department at an Edinburgh High School. I will miss her both as a friend and a bridge to her country and people. Meanwhile, I must help her and her sisters with their English so they can pass their exams.

I haven't heard from my admirer or my last lover, Ernst, who wrote that he had no right to hold on to me. A "Dear John" letter? This is the longest time I have been without male companionship and I miss it.

(Friday 16 June)

My boss' left last week for three month's home leave in the States (which is given after two years at a post). His temporary replacement has arrived and there's no room for him to sit in our tiny, crowded office. He's younger than I expected, speaks beautiful French and is talkative and full of plans.

Last night I entertained him at a dinner party. I invited Luis and Milu, my Irish friend, Kathleen, and the new bachelor in ICA. Not a word of English was spoken and the conversation was so stimulating the guests didn't leave until 1:30 a.m.

The weather has turned humid. Very tiring. Thank goodness my work load has eased. I'm becoming almost human in the office, now that I'm not under pressure and overworked. My poor boss has put up with a lot from me. I shall miss him.

(Sunday 25 June)

I dreamed of India last night and woke up this morning with a cold, empty space inside. The way I used to feel during those last few months after Ernst left. This emotion is rare now, having spent itself during those last months in India and again in Paris before we parted. Forever? But if I'd married Ernst I might have ended up like my English friend Vera, who married a brilliant Indian, Cambridge-educated lawyer. He lost his first case in India and never tried another. Her courage and strength to stay with him and even support him financially is admirable. He makes her happy and she truly loves him. I don't think I could do it and for that reason I sent Ernst back to Argentina, where he had last lived before he went to work in Paris as a UNESCO simultaneous translator.

(Friday 30 June)

When my new boss asked me what I was going to do with my freedom after I resigned, I said, "Lots of interesting things, but mainly I just want to be ME". God knows what the real **ME** is like. Down underneath the layers of self-discipline and duty to do what is expected of me, I might find nothing, but I want to discover it for myself. I can always go on working until I'm sixty, but I might never again have the courage to call "time out".

(Sunday 2 July)

I have become fat (120 pounds), jolly and lazy and have had my hair chopped off to add to the freedom of 'letting go'. I already feel free now that I have decided to cast off the ball and chain. The walls have grown bearable. Yet I'm not blinded to the few pleasures at hand, my silent Sundays, lying in bed reading, listening to music while painting. Just enjoying the silence of my house.

(Tuesday 4 July)

Three hundred, of the four hundred people invited, came to our Embassy Fourth of July party and I think it was a great success. Among the guests were foreign diplomats, high-ranking Senegalese Government officials, and all Americans living in Dakar. The food was excellent, prepared by Embassy wives and served by their teenage sons and daughters. There was even a hotdog stand, which amused the foreigners. At the end of the party the African ballet performed traditional Senegalese dances. By nine-thirty I was exhausted. Standing for three hours, in high heels, while making polite conversation, mostly in French, is both physically and mentally tiring.

(Thursday 6 July)

I want to wake up in the mornings knowing that my only duty is to myself. Since an early age I have been taught that my first duty is to my fellowman, second duty is to work and responsibility, third duty is to myself. This is all very well, but I've found that my duties to fellowman, work and responsibility are never finished. And, too, a lot of "fellow women" can be damned selfish and demanding without giving anything in return. My work doesn't give much satisfaction, mostly because I feel a lot of it is unnecessary. In the end I have to turn to myself for salvation.

(Saturday 8 July)

My headache has finally stopped after three days. On Tuesday I received a letter from the Big Boss in Washington. He stated that he was not pleased to hear of my intentions to give up my job in Dakar. He added that it was doubtful that I would be given a year's leave of absence and I should reconsider my decision. I reconsidered, but I couldn't bring myself to change my decision. No matter the consequences, I must have a break before continuing on the home stretch of thirteen years before retirement.

I have hardly slept for the past few nights and there were moments I felt my courage weaken, but finally, yesterday afternoon I wrote the fatal letter saying that I had not changed my mind. I didn't try to explain my need for a year's leave. My reasons would most likely be misunderstood and the conclusion would be that I was unstable, thus easing their conscience in dismissing me with no further consideration.. Spiritual and psychological needs are still suspect, in spite of the fact that America leads the world in use of psychiatry. As a result everyone has become an amateur psychiatrist and can easily diagnose your case and categorize you in a few moments. I suspect their diagnosis of me would be: A frustrated old maid, or "She's just going through the change," even though I'm only thirty-eight years old.

(Sunday 9 July)

My headache is back. I never learn to slow down. Yesterday, after working half a day at the office, I had a lunch guest, one of "our" officers on his way to Conakry, (Communist) Guinea, to take up his new post. (Poor guy!) After a big meal and lots of good wine we went to the beach and slept it off in the sun and then refreshed ourselves with a long swim in the cool water. Afterwards I went on to a christening party for a young American couple's new baby boy. Then I gathered friends to go to an African party.

It was 10:30 by the time we arrived. There were about fifty young Africans, many of whom I knew, about five French and our little group of five. I had a good chance to practice the Cha-cha-cha, which the Senegalese do very well. It was uncomfortably hot and the humidity took the curl out of my hair, while the African women's fancy hairdos kinked up. When I left at two o'clock the party was still going strong. Probably lasted all night. At least until the Coca-Cola and orange pop finished.

I was supposed to play tennis this morning, but it was pouring with rain. Thank goodness! I was able to sleep until nine o'clock. By noon the sky had cleared. I collected American Pat, drove to the beach where we met British Pat and her colleagues from the British Embassy: Peg (a very proper, attractive English woman a few years older than me whose husband was killed in WWII), Reggie (on Temporary Duty), and Keith (one of few eligible bachelor in the diplomatic corps).

I used to be afraid of deep water unless I could see the bottom, as in swimming pools. But in Cyprus, where the Mediterranean was crystal clear, I overcame that fear, with a little help from a handsome Yugoslav. Even so, I was never a strong swimmer. But today I took up the challenge of the two Pats, and Keith.

We hired a boat that took us across the calm lagoon to a tiny island where we sat on the beach and picnicked on cold chicken, salad, Camembert cheese, French bread, mangoes, and a half bottle of wine each.

Keith suggested we send our clothes back with Peg and Reggie in the boat and then swim across the lagoon, about half a mile. I agreed, feeling overconfident on wine, and the four of us dove into the water.

In sunlight the water was a beautiful deep blue, but soon

clouds slowly spread across the sky and the wind freshened. I could no longer see either the island or the beach. The two Pats were far out in front, Keith was in between, keeping an eye on me, knowing I wasn't a strong swimmer. Slowly panic's icy fingers gripped me. It must have shown on my face, because Keith waited until I caught up with him. In a calm, beautiful voice, he told stories, made me laugh and soon I relaxed, but my arms and legs were giving out. He wanted me to hold on to him, but I was too proud to admit defeat. Through sheer will power I kept on until I could touch bottom and wade ashore, where I collapsed in an exhausted heap on the cold, wet sand.

The beach was empty. Peg and Reggie had gone, taking with them, by mistake, my belongings, including my car keys. The sun had set. My teeth chattered until Keith rummaged in his duffel bag and out came a plastic fold-up raincoat. After about an hour Peg discovered her mistake and drove back with my clothes and car keys.

(Tuesday 11 July)

Heavy, leaden, intense heat is upon us. Our working hours have changed to 0800-1300 Monday through Saturday. This only means that I'm working longer hours than usual. My temporary boss is hopeless at running the office and leaves it to me. Amy is free for the summer and I have a French lesson every morning at eight before I go to work.

(Friday 14 July)

Today is Bastille Day, still celebrated in Senegal, no longer a French colony! Our embassy is closed. I had to get up anyhow at 6:30 to reach the riding stables by seven. A good bracing ride along the beach with British Pat gave me time to think about the letter I received from my "admirer" in Washington.

He wrote: "I am going to do what you should, i.e. get married."

He went on to say that the woman in question was a widow with ten-year-old twin boys; that he was not "bowled over" by the idea, but thought it was sensible; that I gave him a great deal more than I would ever know and for that he was grateful, but he was afraid the difference in age would not make for a good and lasting marriage. I felt sad and wished, momentarily, that I had gone back to Washington. If I ever find a younger version of him there will be no hesitation. Magda wrote that Ernst was back in Buenos Aires and that he would write when he sorted himself out. I don't expect to hear from him again.

(Tuesday 18 July)

I feel much calmer now that I have made a tremendous decision that will change my life even without knowing the outcome. I hope my leave without pay will be approved although it means staying until next year. If the leave is not approved I will resign.

(Sunday 30 July)

We are in the rainy season. My garden is a jungle and the surrounding desert is a green velvet carpet. The nights are sometimes cool, but humidity is high when the sun comes out.

My Portuguese friends, Luis and Milu, are here unofficially. Diplomatic relations between Dakar and Portugal have been broken. The Portuguese Charge d'Affaires and his staff have left. For the time being Luis is here as a tourist. He might be named Consul and remain in that capacity. They would really like another post.

(Tuesday 1 August)

A letter from my boss today. He feared that no amount of persuasion would secure for me a year's leave without pay. Again he begged me to reconsider staying until my tour of duty ends. I hate to disappoint him, but my decision to leave as soon as I can be replaced is stronger each day. I will miss my lovely house, but since it has no romantic memories I can leave it easier. I hope I can get away by Christmas so I can spend the holidays with Lena and Grant in Germany. I keep hearing from Josephine about all the little inexpensive places to stay in Spain and Portugal where I could live cheaply.

(Friday 4 August)

My dinner party last night was interesting. There were five of us. American Pat and a young African couple whose recent wedding I attended, and myself. (A charming Nigerian couldn't come because he was working at a conference which didn't end until midnight.) The Africans didn't speak English and Pat doesn't understand French so I had to do a lot of interpreting, which was a burden on top of having to be hostess. The African couple were Catholic so they could join in cocktails. As always Mamadou gave us a delicious meal: Clams in sauce, rare roast beef, cream potatoes, salad course, cheese course, fresh peaches in cream, white and red wine, and coffee. We talked until midnight. I drove the couple back to the University where he is getting his law degree. His wife has already finished her teacher's training course. It was a pleasant evening and I made friends for my country. I was the first American they had met and they admitted that they were not admirers of the U.S. before meeting me. I was just doing my job as a diplomat. I hope my next effort will be as successful.

I'm giving a farewell party for Amy and I've asked her to invite all her friends, some of whom I know are not fond of the U.S. because of the way black people are treated, but maybe that's because they have never met a U.S. citizen. Maybe I can convert them

(Saturday 5 August)

The party was a great success. The few young men who had

had reservations about coming to my house went away impressed by what they said was my sincerity. They could see the bond between Amy and her sisters and me. Americans, so they thought, waved the stars and stripes and bragged about their great country and how rich they were. "You are different," one of them said. "You seem genuinely interested in our country and culture."

(Monday 7 August)

Amy wanted me to spend her last evening with her and her family (father, mother and 13 children). Being of the wealthier class her father was educated in France. She was feeling sad. I stayed talking to them until almost midnight. I am probably the only white American in the Embassy who has ever been invited into a local family. Amy was thrilled with my going-away presents; gold earrings, a Pan-American zipper bag filled with bits and pieces of new underwear I found in my trunk, especially a panty girdle. For the first time she will wear stockings. The Scottish winters are cold.

(Tuesday 8 August)

Early this morning I went to the airport to see Amy off. It was steaming hot, but she was wearing her first wool suit. August is cool in Europe. Her family and friends seemed happy that I had come.

And now I've just had a lovely horseback ride through the park, green after the rain. On the way back to the stables we rode along the beach. I'm dead tired, but, alas, I've got to change my clothes and drive out to the suburbs to see what Jackie wants. It's getting more difficult to be patient with her. She has a no-good husband, who lives off her income, while carrying on with a local French prostitute. And she can't leave him because she is afraid of being alone! What a joke. She is left alone every night, practically locked in their little house in the native quarters, while he goes to see his mistress. She wants me to keep some of her prized possessions while she is on leave in France. She doesn't trust her husband.

(Saturday 12 August)

Last night I rushed home and dressed for a dinner party at the British Embassy before going to collect Jackie and her kitchen appliances and blankets to hold for safekeeping until she returns from France. I was a bit cross because she brought along her husband. On the way to the port we stopped at my house to leave her belongings. When her ship left I gave a sigh of relief and went on to the dinner party.

After much good food and wine, I finally got away about midnight. I was so sleepy and exhausted I could hardly keep my eyes open long enough to drive myself home.

I parked my little car on the wide sidewalk, tumbled out, dragged myself to the gate, fumbled with the key and finally opened the heavy metal gate. Automatically I locked it behind me and turned toward the house. Something was wrong. Suddenly I was stone sober and afraid.

Ahead through shadows in the garden I saw the front porch door swinging in the wind. I started toward the steps leading up to the door when suddenly it struck me. Someone might be waiting for me in the dark house. In a flash I turned and ran back to the gate. I could almost feel someone behind me as my trembling hand seemed to take forever to unlock the gate. Slamming it behind me I ran as fast as I could.

My high-heeled sandals threatened to fall off with each step as I ran a block up the dark, deserted street and then across to the apartment building where Luis and Milu lived. I flew up two flights of stairs and banged on their door, my heart racing from exertion and fear. Finally Luis, in his bathrobe and still half asleep, opened the door.

"What's wrong?" His eyes, behind thick glasses, looked

enormous with surprise to see me. He beckoned me inside and quickly closed the door.

"Oh, Luis, someone has broken into my house. The front porch door is wide open." I caught my breath. "Someone might be inside."

"Have a seat." He motioned toward a heavy overstuffed chair. "I'll get dressed and go back with you."

Milu appeared in her pale blue negligee and poured me a brandy.

After relating what I had seen, I felt calmer and went with Luis back to my house. Before we reached the steps, he picked up the heavy two-by-four, used by the thief to smash the door in. Cautiously he climbed the steps and tiptoed across the porch. The front door, with a broken lock, stood wide open. Brandishing the wooden club Luis stepped inside and turned on the light.

In the middle of the room sat an open, empty suitcase. Piles of clothes lay scattered over the floor. All my trunks were open and half emptied of new clothes. My two year's supply of underwear gone. Dining room buffet drawers open and linen scattered on the floor. The silver drawer was empty. That was proof enough. So we went to the police station. A young policeman on night duty directed us into the African Commissar's office.

We stated our case. The Commissar said that there had been another burglary in the same neighborhood at 9:30 that night. He showed us a piece of glass with blood on it from the other burglary. The owner of the apartment had surprised the thief before he could leave with suitcases of loot and in getting away he cut himself on a broken window pane.

The Commissar took down our information and then with three policemen he came with us to my house to investigate. I was in such a state of shock when I saw the rest of the rooms, all ransacked, that I could not tell what had been stolen, although it was quite evident that three of my suitcases had been packed up and taken away. The biggest relief was that the thieves hadn't found my best jewelry, stored in a bottom desk drawer, and they had overlooked a case of silverware. But the most maddening thing was that the jacket to my new Paris suit had been taken, along with fourteen sweaters and all my best dresses (even the one I'd worn to the office that day). Oddly enough my two-year supply of new bras were missing. In a country where bras aren't worn! Maybe like sunglasses, bras are a status symbol.

The police took hours to make notes and diagrams. By the time they left I was too tired and angry to find a place to sleep for the night (Luis and Milu have only one bedroom and no sofa). I decided to stay in the house and if someone came I would gladly kill them with my Number Two iron, which I removed from my golf bag and placed beside my bed.

With no locks on the doors to protect me, I slept lightly. The least noise sounded like someone walking barefoot across the marble floor.

This morning when Mamadou arrived the sight of the house sent him into shock. He kept walking from room to room, staring at the empty drawers and piles of clothing on the floor, shaking his head and mumbling something in his native language. Even the spare bed had been torn apart, as though the burglar expected to find a pile of cash hidden under the mattress. It was interesting that out of Jackie's belongings only a blanket had been taken. And even more interesting a suitcase full of clothes, left by a colleague who was traveling in the area, had not been touched!

I spent a couple of hours at the police station giving a list of missing items. My temporary boss was sufficiently influential to get the big White Chief (a Frenchman) to take the case and I must say I felt better. This afternoon he came to look for fingerprints on remaining silver and the clothes in my closet. When he saw blood on a suit jacket he said that probably confirmed his suspicion that the same burglar who had cut himself in another robbery had broken into my house.

After the Police Chief left I tried to have a nap, but people kept ringing up, telling me how sorry they were and offering to lend me something to wear. I had to borrow a bra. The only one I had was black, the one I was wearing the night of the robbery. I gave up trying to rest and kept a tennis date, hoping it would relax me. I also kept a dinner engagement with the American Cultural Affairs officer, an elderly bachelor. Although I'm able to lock the house to a certain degree, I will not feel safe until the porch door is repaired and made stronger.

(Sunday 13 August)

I didn't even have time to straighten up the house before having to go to the office to take care of cable traffic. And then after a four-hour lunch with Amy's family I felt sick. African food is heavy and one has to eat enormous helpings to be polite. Even so, I kept my tennis date with British Pat, who is leaving next week. Then I had to go to the office to send out a dispatch. On the way home I stopped to see Luis and Milu. I was supposed to eat dinner with them, but I was too exhausted.

(Monday 14 August)

Sheer emotional and physical exhaustion caught up with me and I slept eight hours last night, but I still have a tense headache.

There is little hope of getting any of my things back. I will ask my boss to bring me a couple of suitcases when he returns from home leave. A friend will send me some more bras. I never did find anyone in the Embassy who wore my bra size, 32A, slightly bigger than a training bra. I finally got a 34A and stuffed it with Kleenex. I am already known as the "The woman without the Maidenform." It's a good thing it's not sweater weather. Wouldn't matter. I have none left.

Wonder if the burglar has figured out that my sunglasses are prescription? He might be gaining prestige, but he's ruining his eyes. I mourn most my Paris suit. I'll have to replace the blanket Jackie left in my care. What would I do if I smelled Channel No.

5 on a woman at a party? Or if I saw slim feet in my new navy blue pumps. Not many women wear size eight AA.

It's a lovely windy night with the sound of rustling leaves and patches of light from the street where the burglar broke the lattice work out of the door.

(Saturday 19 August)

British Pat is packed and ready to go. She leaves on Monday. She was never happy here, but now that the end is near she feels many regrets and even a bit of sadness. I shall miss her. There are farewell parties for her practically every night this week. By the time she leaves we will be exhausted and tired of seeing one another.

Yesterday I went to the airport with Amy's sister Penda to see another sister, Poupette, off to Pairs.

I feel safer now. My front doors have been repaired and now have stronger locks. The prospect of getting back any of my stolen goods grows dimmer each day.

(Monday 21 August)

A letter from the big boss in Headquarters arrived today. In essence it stated: "Your request for leave has been disapproved and if you cannot continue working without periodic leaves of absence it might be better if you resigned. However, it continued, if you reapplied for employment with the intention of working without undue interruption, your application would be considered." The harshness of this reply was devastating.

He asked for a definite decision, which I will send in the next diplomatic pouch. This letter makes it easy. My resignation is more sensible than ever.

Our hours have changed yet again: 0800-1300 and 1500-1800. No more working on Saturday! The Embassy looks less like a junior high school since the diplomats' teenage children have returned to school in the States.

When I probe my feelings on the eve of resigning I find it difficult to sever all ties with a way of life I have been leading for the past seventeen years. But when I probe deeper I find hope that a year of freedom will renew my spirit and I can continue working until retirement age. I have made no definite plans beyond leaving Dakar. I will face that stage of my new adventure when I have a departure date. I don't even know if the government will pay my way home. I should have thought of that before I decided to resign, but I didn't want financial problems to intimidate me. I am under rigid self-control lest I lose my courage. My main goal for the coming year is gathering knowledge to replenish the empty well inside me. My soul needs freedom to reinforce itself and bring me peace.

(Thursday 24 August)

Today is a Moslem holiday. I have been here one year today! I had hoped to celebrate my anniversary at the beach, but I have to go to the office for a few hours. I have been feeling sick for the past few days and would be quite happy just to lie in bed. We had a terrific rainstorm last night. Thank goodness it rains only at night now, but I can already feel the heat and humidity mounting.

(Friday 25 August)

I've had a headache ever since the thief stole my prescription sun glasses. I wonder if he has noticed that things are a bit out of focus. Sunglasses are such a status symbol that some of the men wear them at night. Worse than Hollywood phonies.

(Saturday 26 August)

American Pat and I came to Dakar about the same time. During the past six months we have drifted apart; she is younger and has her own friends. To celebrate we went to the beach for old time's sake. On the drive along the ocean we recalled the hope we had last year about our future here. We agreed that we had learned a lot, but on the whole the year had been a failure. She resigned last February, but when she found out that she would have to repay the government for her passage to Dakar she canceled her resignation. It is easy to see why morale among the single women in the Embassy is so low. They have no social life, except parties among themselves. There are no eligible bachelors in the Embassy. They don't speak French and even if they did I doubt that they would be interested in cultivating either the French or Africans, as I have. There is nowhere close by of any interest to "get away to". The Senegalese go to France, but few of us can afford the trip. Our high cost of living allowances gives most people the opportunity to save enough money to have a proper holiday in Europe or the Canary Islands on their way back to the States. Even our new Ambassador said that he felt "closed in" and had every intention of either changing the tour of duty to eighteen-months, or sending the staff on holidays to compensate for the boredom here. A two-year tour is too long. It's good to have an Ambassador who is concerned with his staff's morale. We single people are taken for granted. If a husband goes away on business all the wives ban together and take care of the poor wife. But they never notice that we live a lonely life.

(Sunday 27 August)

I lay awake most of the night thinking about my decision to quit. Since I was told that my application would be considered if I decided to return I finally soothed myself with the reasoning that I would be of more value to the Agency with the knowledge of French (and maybe Spanish), a new outlook, and determination to serve out the remainder of my time. I can't make definite plans until my replacement arrives and I know the amount of money I will have at my disposal. I pray that after eight years outside the U.S. the government will send my household effects home and pay my way. I still think it was a wise decision and I'm willing to bear the consequences.

I'm still doing my bit to make African friends for my country. Although it is trying at times, the results turn out well. Last night I gave a dinner party for President Senghor's Chief of Arabic Affairs and rumored to be their next ambassador to Morocco. He was a lot more difficult than most of my acquaintances, because he is physically unattractive, very complex and a bit hostile toward America. But thanks to the support of my other guests, especially Luis and Milu, the evening turned out quite successfully. It is easier to be a hostess in French than it is to be a guest. As hostess I can choose the right kind of guests, feed them well, direct the conversation and then sit back and enjoy the results. As a guest I have to participate more. I hope my successor will be interested in the Senegalese and can reap the profits of my spade work. This is their country now. Not the French. When I arrived, just as Senegal became independent, our diplomats had few, if any, African friends. When the French left we had a hard time getting Senegalese to attend our diplomatic receptions. Even now I'm one of the few who has Senegalese friends. I've promised my Ambassador, a former professor, to introduce him to my Senegalese student friends. I still find it difficult to remember their faces. For that reason I got myself into a real bind a few days ago.

I was unlocking my garden gate when I glanced up at a tall Senegalese man walking toward me on the sidewalk. Through my mind flashed Amy's comment: "My friends say that you never speak to them on the street." I didn't want to tell her that sometimes I didn't recognize them. So as I looked at the man approaching I thought he appeared familiar, so I said, *"Bonjour."* His face lit up and he returned the greeting with enthusiasm.

I finished unlocking the gate as we exchanged a few words. He seemed reluctant to move on. Thinking he was one of Amy's many University friends, and being a victim of race-discrimination guilt, I invited him to come in for tea.

When we entered the living room I noticed Mamadou's

puzzled expression, but dismissed it as I thought he, too, would soon recognize Amy's friend. Even before we had been served tea I realized that this man was not Amy's friend, but there was nothing I could do but carry on. As we drank tea and ate cookies he told me that he was a government clerk. He didn't know Amy or any of her friends. He said that he lived in the apartment building across the street and used to watch me from his balcony.

"I've always wanted to meet you," he said. "Imagine my surprise," he added, grinning, "when you invited me to tea."

Not only was I mortified, I realized that Mamadou had gone out to market and I was alone with this total stranger. I remembered the stigma attached to single women living alone. We were thought of as women of easy virtue. Was that what he was thinking as his eyes took in every inch of me.

I looked at my watch and said that my roommate would soon be coming home, but somehow I knew that he knew that I didn't have a roommate. I willed the phone to ring, anything for an excuse to get this man out of my house. Finally I said I had to return to the Embassy and stood up. He rose to his feet and approached me with his hand outstretched. When I shook his hand he pulled me to him and I froze.

His face contorted, anger shot from his dark eyes and his heavy lips twisted into a smirk. "All the time I thought you might be different," he tightened his grip around my waist, "but you're just like all the Americans. You hate blacks." With that he shoved me away and stalked out.

From then on I decided that I'd rather be known as a snob than to have another unpleasant experience as it was for both of us.

(Tuesday 29 August)

Life rushes by with the same distractions week in and week out. Cocktail parties, dinner parties, 9:00 p.m. movies, old American films with French subtitles or dubbed in French (I still can't get used to John Wayne speaking French). Beaches, tennis, horseback riding and golf. There are not many places in the world where a mere working woman can have such an active life and such luxuries; comfortable villa/flat, an excellent servant to do all the cooking and household slogging. Meanwhile I'm learning French. So what is wrong? The answer comes quickly: no male companionship. I need a man who has the same interests and can share all this with me. A man who can share ideas and enjoy discovering this strange country with me.

Letter from Jackie. She has arrived home in Normandy, but the burden of her husband hovers over her. She wanted me to give him 5,000 Francs. Luckily I haven't been able to find him. He called me at the office a couple of days ago and said he had a job outside Dakar and would I keep their big dog. I told him that I was in the middle of a conference and to call me at home. He never called again, thank goodness. I don't like the way he treats Jackie. I think he burgled my house. He knew I was going to be out until about midnight. Also it was interesting that of all the valuable possessions Jackie left with me, the burglar took only a blanket.

At Jackie's request I took time to drive to the Medina, where the poorer Senegalese live, to check on her little shack of a house. The gate was open and the dog was not there. Her husband has probably gone to St. Louis. To sell stolen loot? Poor Jackie. How long will she put up with such treatment.

(Thursday 31 August)

American Crossroads volunteers working in (communist) Guinea appeared at the Embassy and I was asked to introduce them to my African friends. They were a charming group of dedicated Americans working to promote better understanding between young people throughout the world. Among them was Norman Cousins' daughter. I trotted out my friends to meet them, provided plenty to eat and drink and sat back and listened. The

Crossroaders spoke excellent French. The Senegalese were more anti-Sekou Toure than the Crossroaders, who praised the Guinean peoples' enthusiasm and work for the betterment of their country. I wondered if the Crossroaders might be a bit naive about Toure. It takes an African to know an African.

(Monday 4 September)

Labor Day. Today was spent taking Amy's sisters, Poupée and Peneta , to the beach with the intention of teaching them to swim. As a rule Africans don't go to the beach, but recently I have noticed a sprinkling of bikini-clad locals self-consciously approach the sea as if afraid. Many of them just paddle in the surf. My success in cultivating young Africans, I believe, is because they genuinely want to learn the pleasures of the white people. I feel that they know that I am serious in my desire to help bridge the gap and therefore they have confidence in me. The French here do not practice segregation, but there is a big gap between them and the Africans. It's ironic that my friends look to me, an American, to give them self-confidence in their own country! I couldn't help noticing that there were many curious glances my way yesterday when I appeared at the beach with five young Africans girls and proceeded to try to teach them to swim. The girls had a good time, but didn't learn to swim, of course. It is the same as teaching them tennis or inviting them to dinner parties, they are very self-conscious until they have gained confidence. They are well educated, well read and intelligent and add a lot to my parties. Sometimes I feel like a matron headmistress. We speak in French, but they call me "Miss McNeill".

Yesterday I received a ten-page letter from Amy. She'd had a hard time after she arrived in Scotland because she couldn't find a place to live, but soon she was surrounded by kind people who wanted to help her. Strange now that she is in a "white" country her family feel drawn to me. They phone me each time they receive a letter and I go to read it and we discuss her problems. I write often to encourage her.

Torrential rains have flooded the tennis courts and golf course. My back garden looks like a lake. There is practically no traffic on the street, in front of my house, which looks like a river. I think of the poor people in the Medina, flooded out of their hovels.

Here I sit comfortably drinking a cup of coffee and talking to my diary, untouched by the cruel elements. I don't even have to get my feet wet getting into my car because I am on holiday and as soon as I finish this entry I can go back to bed and read all morning. After a year here I'm taking a whole week of leave.

Jacqueline's husband finally came to see me after I left a note under his door. He said he'd been out in the "bush" and assured me that the dog was quite happily living with a friend who has a garden. All dressed up in his blue suit and carrying a little overnight case, he looked the picture of health. He said he'd even gained weight. I'm sure someone is taking care of him. He had a drink with me. I gave him 3,000 Francs. He will come later for the remaining 2,000 of the 5,000 Frs Jackie sent me. I urged him to talk about himself so I could find out what he was up to, but he wanted to talk about my burglary (little did he know I suspected him). He said he hadn't heard from Jackie and feared her letters were being taken from their mail box. I told him that she hadn't heard from him either, but he swore that he had been writing. (I didn't believe him, but I bet she does.) After he left I wrote to Jackie and assured her that she need not worry about him starving. I told her that he hoped to get a job in the "bush"..doing what, I couldn't find out.

(Tuesday 5 September)

A letter that will never be sent: "Dear Ernst, The sea rages and the tortured lemon tree, outside my window, bends to the wind and sheds its fruit, like giant, yellow tear drops among the wet, black pebbles in the garden. It's another magnificent storm.

"Yesterday I stood on the cliff, near the lighthouse, watching the angry, purple waves hurl themselves against the red clay and then recede bloody and defeated. The stinging salt spray brought memories of our early morning walks along the sea wall in Bombay. I thought of you and your love for the sea. Again today I think of you and wonder if the storm within you is still raging. Is it? Or are you riding the crest of the waves. Waiting.

"I, too, have been waiting, waiting a long time for your letter. Even a *"Bonjour"* in your familiar handwriting would be a pleasure. I've given up hope of a detailed account of your activities, thoughts, and plans since we parted two long years ago. I sense that you are still going through the valley of the shadow, but please speak to me. Say something.

"Most of the recent happenings in my life have been insignificant. I work less hard and play more. I have developed a passion for tennis. I entertain with hopes that my guests enjoy themselves. I am entertained and try to be a good guest. I read, mostly in French. I have just finished *Climats*, by Andre Maurois. I continue to eat well, especially fresh fish from the sea behind my house. I succumb more often to my cool bedroom as the weather gets hotter and more humid. I drift.

"What about you? Will I meet you on some distant shore, or will the thread between us grow longer and eventually break?"

(Thursday 7 September)

In another letter to Jacqueline I tried to make her see that her husband was playing on her sympathy when he told her he was living off bread, water and cheese. I scolded her about supporting him, not insisting that he get a job and take a husband's responsibility. I've hinted that he probably has a mistress, but she is so blinded by love she can't see through him.

(Saturday 9 September)

Ruth, the new Ambassador's secretary is a great addition to the staff. She is attractive, of Swedish extraction, well-educated, disciplined, can't stand superficiality, and doesn't abide fools gladly. In other words we feel alike on most subjects. She is about my age and an old "Pro", having served in many foreign countries. She is disappointed, as I am, in the leadership of top diplomats. We are constantly dismayed at their provincialism, their weakness as administrators, their lack of interest in Senegal and its people.

This morning we went to play tennis, but the court at the beach was flooded so, instead, we spent the morning sunning, swimming and talking. I told her that I had resigned. At first she was shocked, then she said she wished she had the courage to do the same, but she wouldn't know what to do with herself for a whole year! She, too, is turning into a pinched-faced, bad-tempered Government-Girl Monster in the office, which often happens to intelligent women who will not settle for mediocrity. Not only do we demand a great deal of ourselves, we demand the same of others. We know that many of them have nothing more to give, but we can't adjust our expectations so we react by becoming critical and sarcastic.

As Spanish philosopher Ortega y Gasset said, "There are two classes of men; those who make great demands on themselves, piling up difficulties and duties; and those who demand nothing special of themselves, but for whom to live is to be every moment what they already are, without imposing on themselves any effort towards perfection."

(Sunday 10 September)

I took Penda to lunch at the posh N'Gor Hotel. At first she was nervous and self-conscious with all the white people staring at her, but soon she seemed at ease and gained some self-confidence. It was sad to see her feel inferior in her own country. In the evening she and her three sisters took me to the cinema and this time I was the odd "white".

In a letter from my boss (on leave in Washington, D.C.), he praised my work and said he was désolé to lose me and that I could work for him again anytime I wanted to. He arranged return passage for me and my household effects, but he couldn't get me a year's leave without pay. I will be glad when he returns. His temporary replacement is incompetent.

I have finished reading *Revolt of the Masses* by Ortega y Gasset. None of my stolen goods has been found and I have no insurance.

(Friday 22 September)

I've just worked nine hours in this devastating heat and humidity. At least I have mastered the electric typewriter and now couldn't do without it. Its speed has cut in half the time I spend typing out coded and decoded messages and writing intelligence reports, not to mention administrative work.

And now I have to get dressed for a scrabble party at the British Embassy. Afterwards, no matter how late, I will have to come home, change clothes, grab my toothbrush, toiletries, etc. and summon up strength to drive out to Point E, thirty minutes away, and spend the night with Camille, who is afraid to stay alone. Her husband, one of "us", is on temporary duty in Bamako. She has a big German shepherd and lives in an apartment building with five other families, all of whom have dogs. Approaching the building is like walking into a mad dog kennel. Even so, she is terrified to stay alone.

(Saturday)

It was a restless night. Camille has only one bedroom. I slept on the edge of her bed and the four-month-old baby slept in its crib. The small apartment is cramped. There is no airconditioner and no cross ventilation, but I was so tired last night that not even the baby's crying woke me up. This morning I felt lethargic, but dragged myself out of bed, left Camille asleep, dressed and drove home. It was a beautiful morning, the rising sun had spread a faint pink over the sea and the sky.

Mamadou was already there and prepared my breakfast. I was tempted to go to bed, but I had promised Ruth to pay tennis with her at N'Gor. We had lunch there and then I went to the office and took care of cable traffic. Then it was time to dress for Ruth's dinner party, where I met a very attractive Frenchman with the United Nations. Afterwards he invited me to go dancing at the Windsor Bar. Speaking French over the din of amplified band music until three o'clock in the morning gave me a dreadful headache. Thank goodness I had called Camille and begged off spending the night because I had got my period.

(Sunday)

Last night, suffering from menstrual cramps, I had just fallen into a deep sleep when the phone rang. It was 5:00 a.m. and the voice I heard, through a thundering headache was Camille's. "I'm desperately ill. Could you please come?"

Half asleep and my head throbbing, I somehow made it out to Point E, along the narrow coastal road in the dark.

Poor Camille's migraine was so fierce that she couldn't even sit up, so I had to take over. The rest of the day was a blur. I had to feed and bathe the baby, cook the dog's food and walk him. Having had no experience with such a tiny baby I was constantly worried that I would do something wrong. With all the tension and stress, added to the unbearable heat of the apartment, I felt on the verge of a heat stroke. After I finally got the baby to sleep I eased down on the edge of Camille's bed, but I was too exhausted to sleep. It's just as well. I was up several times to feed and change the baby.

(Monday)

Camille was no better this morning. She had vomited until there was nothing left in her stomach. We tried, in vain, to get a doctor. His home phone number was unlisted. We waited until his office opened. The nurse said he didn't make house calls. We would have to bring the patient in. I called an embassy officer, who said he would take her to the doctor. I got her dressed and he carried her down two flights of stairs (and back up when they returned) and drove her into town. The doctor gave her a shot and lots of sleeping pills.

She got little relief and suffered terribly all day. I've taken care of the baby and tried to help ease her pain. I stay bathed in perspiration and smell like baby's vomit. My bones are weary. I can't even lie down while the baby sleeps. I could fall asleep in a chair, if there was a comfortable one here. About two o'clock a friend of Camille's relieved me so that I could go home, take a bath, check the office for messages to be answered. Since my boss left on home leave I've had to practically run the office. His substitute is hopeless. On the way back to Camille's I stopped by my apartment and picked up food Mamadou had prepared for our dinner.

(Tuesday)

One of the embassy wives relieved me today so that I could do my office work. I had to spend the day encoding and decoding a backlog of messages, typing them out and then writing answers to some of them. No time for lunch. After work I took time to get my hair chopped off. It's not very becoming, but I can no longer manage it in this hot weather while living as I do. By the time I rushed by my house, picked up food Mamadou had prepared, and got back out to Point E, the embassy wife was champing at the bit to get away. She said she couldn't come the next day, but she had arranged for another wife to come.

(Wednesday)

After another sleepless night I had to wait until ten o'clock for the "other" wife, by which time I had bathed and fed the baby, fed Camille, cooked food for the dog and walked him. I was already exhausted and my dress damp and smelly. I had to go by my house, take a bath and put on a fresh dress, give Mamadou instructions for an evening meal. Camille being picky about her food makes it difficult to plan a menu. I told Mamadou that I would be home for lunch, after which I would have an hour's rest. But, alas, just before noon the embassy wife called and said that she wanted to go home and have lunch with her family!! I couldn't believe it. I told her it would be a great favor to me if she could stay, but she said she couldn't do it, she would "try", she said, to get back to Camille about three o'clock! I wanted to say, "forget it!" I took my lunch and shared it with Camille and we decided to call her husband to come home. That, too, was an experience. Finally we got through to his secretary, but she couldn't locate him. She said she would scour the town, find him and have him call. He didn't, which set Camille to worrying.

(Thursday)

Fatigue is building. I left Camille alone, after doing all the chores and taking care of the baby, and came to the office to use our official phone to contact her husband. I spent an hour on the phone before I finally reached him. He said he would be on the plane the following day. Could I meet him at the airport? "And by the way," he added, "could you transfer my official dinner party from my house to yours tomorrow night and notify all the guests." There went my hope for a free night to catch up on my sleep.

(Saturday)

All is well! Camille's husband returned yesterday. I met him at the airport and got him settled at home. Camille was relieved. He presented me with a magnificent carved African bust from the Bamako Museum.

By the time he and his guests, Senegalese officials, arrived at my house for dinner, everything was ready. The party was a success, but in my fatigued state (after a grueling day at the office) I had to concentrate hard to understand their French. When the last guest left I fell into bed and slept nine hours, a miracle for me.

I'm still not rested, but there's no time to enjoy my freedom. This afternoon a crowd of Bamako embassy employees are coming here for rest and recreation. I have offered a bed to one of the secretaries, but if I have a chance I will suggest that, after a year in the interior of Africa, it would be much more exciting to spend their holiday at the beautiful N'Gor Hotel. They can afford it. They get a big allowance. Besides I had already made plans for this weekend.

(Wednesday 27 September)

Another burglary in the neighborhood. The owner of the house was in France so the buglers had plenty of time to completely clean out the house.

Jo was upset that the sari she'd worn at the costume party, given in her honor, had been among the stolen object. She sent me a check for $60.00 to replace some of my sweaters when I go to Europe, but I can't accept it. I will need to stay with her when I return to Washington to look for a job.

The announcement of my retirement will come as a surprise to my colleagues in the embassy. I'm one of the few people who hasn't spent the past year complaining about this dreadful place. I am not a complainer. Either I accept the situation, or I walk away, as I plan to do.

(Monday 9 October)

October is the hottest, most humid month of the year. My Portuguese dressmaker has just left. Thank goodness I found her in time to remodel all the out-of-style dresses left behind by the thief. I even entrusted her with a piece of lovely Indian cotton material. What she does with it will not surprise me. Experience over the years in Japan, Iran, Turkey and India taught me that my interpretation of a magazine picture might not be the same as my dressmaker sees it. It's all in the eye of the beholder, as they say.

Amy's two sisters were invited to come with me to an American embassy party. I had to call their father to get his permission. It was the first time I'd spoken to him by phone. At first he didn't understand me, but after he adjusted to my accent we had a good conversation about Amy and how she had gained weight in Scotland.

There were about twenty of us, including the Ambassador, his wife and an *au pair* girl living with them. Most of the guests were my Senegalese friends from the University. Our embassy still finds it difficult to get Senegalese to come to our diplomatic parties. Many of them, educated in France and married to French women (including President Senghor,) feel, as do the French, culturally superior to Americans. Too, while the French were in charge of the country I've heard that most of our diplomatic invitations went to French officials. Now they are gone and the Senegalese aren't interested. I hope this will change soon. At social functions diplomats can get to know local government officials.

(Tuesday 10 October)

Yesterday I drove to the airport to meet Andre, my university friend. He is not as attractive as my Senegalese friends. His African features are coarser, but being from Ghana, a British colony, he doesn't have that cultural snobbery of the French colons. He speaks good English and I can express myself better with him on political subjects. He has just returned from East Germany, invited by the communists. He looked warm in a tweed jacket. Not having time to hear about his experiences, I left him at the University with promises to get together soon.

(Wednesday 11 October)

It's not even seven o'clock and I've already had my breakfast. I'm going through a period of waking up at dawn with that awful feeling that "all is not well". There's something pressing on my mind. I can't put my finger on it, unless it's the finality of my resignation. I received the official acknowledgment yesterday. It stated that Headquarters was sorry to accept my resignation. At the same time they hoped they could take me at my word to stay on until a replacement is found. It might even be spring before they can get someone out here. I'm not surprised. Who would want to come to French West Africa? They admit that women like me are almost impossible to find, yet they do very little to keep us. Maybe that's the reason the government is top heavy with employees who never need Intellectual replenishment as I do. Many wouldn't know what to do with a whole year of freedom, having little ambition to stretch their mental capacities. After seven years without giving me a raise, they now prevail upon my sense of duty to be patient with their inability to find qualified employees to send to the field, where work is harder and promotions fewer. Every woman I know, of my age, doing the job I do, is at least two grades higher and wouldn't dream of coming to an African post. Much is my fault. I have never asked for a raise. I find it difficult to ask anyone for anything. I always hoped my excellent efficiency reports would be rewarded. Until now, I have enjoyed my life in faraway, exotic countries so much I would have worked for even less.

I have been toting up my savings to see how long I could stretch my sabbatical. I'm astounded. I've saved $5,000.00, because I have little expense other than food and a cook. I've bought no clothes and only a few household items since I've been here.

(Thursday 12 October)

This African heat and humidity, and working in an office without air conditioning, saps my energy. I had to force myself out of bed this morning. I was too active yesterday; Lunch with a girl friend left no time for a siesta. I rushed home after work, washed my hair, put it in rollers and sat under a hair dryer for half hour, got dressed (my underclothes wet before I could get my dress on) and went to The Ambassador's reception. He speaks passable French, but his wife has great difficulty. It was a nice reception, but I got very tired trying to make small talk and moving from group to group. There must have been seventy guests. Luckily the Ambassador's residence, on slightly higher elevation than the city, gets a good breeze.

I left at eight thirty and went to dinner with Luis and Milu; more French. He speaks perfect English, but Milu speaks only French. Their small apartment was hot and stuffy and I ate too much food, but the conversation was lively. Their other guest was a charming Senegalese diplomat who will soon be Ambassador to Yugoslavia. Their parties begin late and last until the wee hours. It was almost two this morning when I got home.

Today I have a heavy schedule and no time for rest. I have a "working" lunch at the National Assembly with a very nice Senegalese, chief of Arabian Affairs and Senegal's next ambassador to Morocco. In the evening I'm having a "working" dinner party to introduce Andre to my temporary boss, who has the notion that he can recruit Andre to work for us.

My effort to favorably represent the U.S.A. has been noted in my efficiency report. Many American diplomats really don't get to know foreigners well enough to make wise foreign policy. I'm always surprised at how many foreign service employees (diplomats included) really don't like foreigners, but they like the life style and all the perks. In stipulating the qualities for my replacement my boss noted that it must be someone with the same talent and enthusiasm I have for getting along well and making friends with the Senegalese.

(Friday 13 October)

About 1:30 this morning my dinner guests left. They were, in addition to Andre and my temporary boss, a young couple from Dahomey. They met in the U.S. where they studied on scholarships and later married in Spain. He returned from America bitter and disillusioned and still smarting from the humiliations suffered from discrimination. However, time and a job in our embassy have dimmed some of those memories.

Andre, the guest of honor and a leftist (yes, I have all sorts of friends), has just returned from Eastern Europe, where he went to see for himself and make up his own mind about communism. From his letters I got the impression, which he confirmed last night, that his eyes were opened to a lot of things he didn't see on his prior trip to Europe to attend the Vienna Peace Conference. His biggest disillusionment with the communists came while he was visiting friends in East Germany. He found out that the educated middle-class could no longer keep the position, for which they had worked hard to attain, because of the leveling-off process. Needless to say, the rich always fare badly in the face of "socialism". After young people complete their education they are sent to work where the State wants them and where they have to stay, like it or not. They have to get permission to visit their family. Traveling within the country is not even allowed, much less going to Paris, or even Moscow. Not only is life hard in the way of material necessities, but there's always that element of fear in a police state.

I gave the dinner party for the express purpose of making Andre say all this in front of my temporary boss. Since Andre had already told me about his disillusionment, he couldn't change his story. He is a loyal leftist and I don't think he would have told my boss about his disillusionment under any other circumstances.

In a way I blackmailed him, but unfortunately that is the CIA game. I felt badly about it, because I knew how hard it was for him to face the reality of communism.

When my temporary boss insisted on the dinner party, with recruitment in mind, I told him that Andre might have been disillusioned in communism, but he wasn't ready to turn against it and become a CIA agent. I pointed out that my friendship had not changed his unfavorable opinion of the U.S.and the way blacks are treated there. After the party my boss never mentioned the subject again. I think he could sense that Andre didn't like him.

(Saturday 14 October)

I met my 'real' boss's plane this morning at four o'clock. It was an hour late, thank goodness. By the time I got him, his wife and four kids home and settled it was six o'clock and still dark. I fell into bed and slept two hours.

It is now ten o'clock. After two hours of tennis I've just finished a big breakfast. It's really too hot to play. One set leaves me weak with fatigue.

I'll go to the office for a couple of hours to brief my boss on what has happened since he's been away. He already knows, from my letters, that his replacement was a dud. He speaks seven languages, which in itself is enough to destabilize anyone. A heavy drinker, he doesn't have any social graces and not a clue as to how to handle people. At the end he rarely came to the office. I didn't blame him. I found it difficult to hold my tongue and not show my disdain when he did something stupid, or when I heard that he spent his evenings at bars, drinking and talking too much.

This afternoon I'll buy myself a real French bikini to wear this evening. I'm going to a picnic on Gorée Island with a group of young French artists, who for some reason have taken a liking to me, especially Charles-Louis, a lively, entertaining young artist who keeps us all laughing. I'm flattered. I like young people, especially artists. Bounette, a sculptress, and Alain, a Naval officer stationed in Dakar, are part of the Charles-Louis group.

(Sunday 15 October)

Bounette arranged for the evening party on Gorée Island, from where African slaves were shipped off, in chains, to Europe and the New World. Relatively small and rocky, it lies about three miles offshore and is reached by a short ferry ride. No cars or bicycles are allowed. It is inhabited by old African families and very few French. Some people keep small weekend flats there. The fishing is good, there is a small beach and one very good restaurant. I assume that most of the first settlers were catholic, judging from the old church in the center of the island. The ferry ride, thirty cents, is the cheapest thing I have found in Dakar.

Bounette, Alain, Charles-Louis , eight of their French friends (all my junior by ten years) and I arrived on the island just after sunset, and deposited our food on two not-so-clean tables in a small African *epicerie*, owned by a friend of someone in our group. After a big glass of white wine we set off in the dark (night falls early here) climbing up and down the rock cliff until we found a safe place to swim.

After a bracing dip in the cool Atlantic, we wrapped ourselves in sarongs of bright-colored local material, sat on Coca-Cola cases around the table and had a banquet. A bottle of wine each dissolved our inhibitions and sent us singing and dancing barefoot on the dirt floor until someone suggested another swim. We raced to the public beach and dove into the dark, cold water. Shivering, we emerged a few minutes later and wrapped ourselves back in our sarongs and lay on blankets, talking and laughing. We caught the last ferry back at one o'clock. Most of us still wrapped in a sarong and barefooted. The party continued, but I begged off.

Lying in bed this morning, looking back over last night, I was shocked at seeing myself, a Lady Diplomat in her late thirties, in a teeny-weeny polka-dotted bikini, dancing barefoot, laughing, flirting and behaving like a twenty-year-old. "What happened to me?" Was I so starved to let my hair down that I lost my perspective? I don't know the answer, but I know that I was attracted to Charles-Louis and it seemed mutual. But it was only a night of fun, which might never be repeated.

I awakened with a headache and wanted to lie in bed and let the rest of the world go by, but fate is not always kind. At eight o'clock my doorbell started ringing.

There with his nose pressed against the grill in the garden gate was the poor gardener whom I've been putting off for weeks because I didn't want to waste my Sundays giving him instructions. I let him in and led him through the house to the back garden (the only way to get there). After hours of pruning, occasionally supervised by me (!) otherwise he would have cut everything down. Gardeners are as ruthless with a pair of pruning shears as a modern hair stylist with scissors. All the cuttings had to be carried through the house. When he finished, I paid him and returned to my study to write letters. Later I went outside to gather the flowers I'd cut. There at the big stone wash basin, in the corner of the garden, stood the gardener busily washing his tunic, seemingly not embarrassed at being naked, except for a loin cloth. He didn't even seem to be aware of my presence and the next thing I knew he was sitting in the sink, bathing. I took him soap and a towel so that he could have a proper bath. Life for the poor is hard in Dakar.

After a piece of cold chicken for lunch I picked up Panda and we went to the beach. She was the only black woman there and a treat to look at in her orange bikini; a magnificent figure with satin black skin. Although a devout Moslem, she is no longer shy about wearing a bikini and seems eager to take off her long flowing robe. I'm not having much luck teaching her to swim, but she loves the water. After swimming we lay on big padded chaise longues under an umbrella. She studied for her law exam and I read *The Revolt of the Masses*. I had to cut our afternoon short and go to the office. Afterwards I had my usual Sunday night dinner with Luis and Milu.

(Tuesday 17 October)

Yesterday I had a long talk with my boss. He asked me to stay until next April. I said I would consider staying until the end of January. I'm eager to get to Europe to ski. I'll have to scratch Christmas plans to ski with Lena and Grant, stationed in Bonn.

(Wednesday 18 October)

In a letter from my sister-in-law, a nurse, she said that nurse's notes, an important part of a patient's medical history, are now being destroyed after the patient is discharged. Does that mean illnesses will now be categorized and punched out in IBM cards? All black and white. No grays. No "mildly depressed", just "depressed." Anything that can't be categorized is of no importance? What about the human spirit? Reactions and emotions? They can't be punched out on IBM machines.

(Saturday 21 October)

It's a wonderful morning with a cool ocean breeze. I almost feel rested in spite of having worked like a mad woman yesterday to get the diplomatic pouch out. I got home last night at 7:15 p.m. so tired I could hardly take a shower and dress before receiving five dinner guest: Luis and Milu, Charles-Louis and Bounette, and a UN official who is French by birth and American by nationality. The best small party I have given. Intelligent guests and lively discussions were the main ingredients. That's probably the reason I feel so good this morning. Many parties are such chores that I don't relax, especially since the conversation is always in French. When Charles-Louis said "Good Night" he kissed me on both cheeks. I'm ashamed to say I felt a thrill. It has been so long since I've had male companionship I must be careful not to loose my perspective. Charles-Louis is much too young for me.

A 'working' Lunch today with an African government official at the National Assembly. Afterwards I will meet an Embassy secretary, visiting from her post in Bamako, take her to the beach and then to a cocktail party after which I'm invited to dinner.

(Sunday 22 October)

The sudden cool weather has brought energy and made me restless. Life is passing me by and I'm helpless to do anything about it. The future is still fuzzy, out of focus.

(Monday 23 October)

I collapsed yesterday, completely exhausted, and slept until this morning. I didn't realize how near I was to a physical breakdown. I tried to wash my hair, but I couldn't even raise my arms so today I went to the beauty parlor, had my hair cut and a permanent and slept through the entire process. The beautician said, "*Vous ête trés fatiguê, n'cest pas?*"

(Wednesday 25 October)

Last night at a British diplomat's birthday party, I met UN Ambassador Nawab Mir Khan, a Pakistani. Hearing him speak "cottonball" English made me homesick for India. After the party he invited Ruth and me to his house for a drink and to listen to his Indian records, which brought waves of nostalgia for a country with which I had a great affinity. It was three o'clock when I got to bed this morning.

(Thursday 26 October)

Overnight the green countryside has turned dry and parched in places. The nights are cool and the sea is almost winter temperature. Social season is gearing up. Last night after the UN Day party, attended by Vice-President Mamadou Dia, my boss and his wife took me to dinner at the L'Escale Restaurant. Best food in town.

(Saturday 28 October)

Thursday I worked until 1:30 a.m. Friday night, after the diplomatic pouch went out I was too tired to have dinner with Luis and Milu, but before I could fall into bed American Pat dropped by for a drink.

This morning the doorbell woke me at 7:30. It was my dressmaker. After a fitting I had breakfast, finished a letter, left in my typewriter, thanking British Pat for a sweater she sent from Scotland. So thoughtful!

Dressed in tennis shorts, I collected my partners Pat and Mary and Betty for doubles, drove to the N'Gor Hotel. We were on the court at 9:00 and off at 10:00. I was at the office by 10:45, worked until 12:45. I then collected Pat, zoomed by my Boss's house, picked up bathing trunks for a "visiting fireman" (one of "us") who was waiting for me at the golf club. Stopped by my house, helped Mamadou pack a picnic lunch, got my golf equipment together, drove Pat to the beach and finally arrived at the Golf Club at 1:30. Picked up said "visiting fireman", who had played golf all morning, drove a few more miles to Camberene Beach. We swam and picnicked on cold roast beef, French bread, camembert cheese, red wine and melon for dessert. We returned to the Golf Club and played nine holes of golf. I then drove him to the N'Gor Hotel (miles out of my way), rushed home, bathed, washed and set my hair, dried it, dressed and rushed out to Point E to a cocktail party given by the assistant UN Director. After one gin-tonic I started feeling really tired, but I still had to go to a "working" dinner party at my Boss' house. By the time I had another gin-tonic and dinner I could hardly hold my head up I was so tired and sleepy. I got into bed at 0100 hours.

(Sunday 29 October)

Today has been just about as hectic. I packed a picnic, played eighteen holes of golf with visitor from Headquarters, and afterwards we went swimming. We had planned to play again in the afternoon but exhaustion overtook us. I came home about five, washed and dried my hair and rushed back out to the N'Gor Hotel to pick up the visitor for an appointment. On the way back I ran out of gas and he was late for his meeting.

(Thursday 2 November)

It's a glorious morning. Cool shadows and patches of sunlight mixed with a fresh wind from the ocean. It's a holiday, but I was up early gathering my tennis mates. We were on the court at eight o'clock and had a good game. I feel mentally and physically alert which is refreshing after so many months of fatigue and lethargy. Winter has come to Dakar and I hope to profit from it during my remaining months here.

(Friday 3 November)

It looks as though I will be here until February. With a definite end in sight, I have started really enjoying my house and the pleasures I have here. Since my boss returned I'm working harder than ever. I should be able to adopt the attitude that I will do what I can within working hours and the rest will have to go undone. But my sense of duty is too deeply ingrained and I'm unable to lower my standards. So I'm in the office seven days a week most of the time.

In the wee, dark hours I was awakened by what sounded like someone walking around in the living room. For a moment I held my breath, listening. After a wave of panic I reasoned that it was the wind blowing a bougainvillea branch across the living room window. I wouldn't have even noticed, but since being burgled I know my house can be broken into.

(Saturday 4 November)

Last night I attended a dinner party given by our Cultural Attaché in honor of young African students going on an orientation tour of America. I felt uncomfortable, knowing their enthusiasm for my country would be destroyed. There is no way they can be sheltered from racism. And like others who have gone before them, they will come back anti-America. I have talked to the Cultural Attaché about my concern, but he says that all the wonderful things about America will cancel out their contact with racists. (I can't think of one single thing that would "cancel out" being humiliated because of skin color.) I gave him examples of my Dakar university friends, who had come back hating the U.S.

In this tug of war between the U.S. and the U.S.S.R. to win the hearts and souls of the students, I suggested that we encourage students to go to the Soviet Union. Let the Soviets pay for travel and we shall see how many return loving the USSR. I also know students who have studied in Moscow. They not only faced discrimination they returned hating the Soviet system of government. In the long run, how important is it for the Senegalese to be pro-American? It's a small, former French colony of not much global importance whose elite have been educated in French Universities and feel themselves intellectually superior to Americans. I say to the American diplomats, show by example that you are not a racist. That's enough. That's what I'm doing. These people read newspapers, they know what goes on in the States. Sending them there, at taxpayers expense, to be humiliated because of their black faces hardly seems a wise thing to do.

(Tuesday 7 November)

I see in the press that the U.S. is swinging toward conservatism. Doesn't surprise me. From afar we look like nation of extremes. I see it in our aid programs. We give billions of dollars to a country, with no strings attached, and then when they don't do what we expect them to do we get mad and cut off the aid. We must be more realistic and clear about what WE want in our relations with other countries. We give you *this* and we want *that* in return. But alas, most of our aid is based on fear of communism (as are most of our actions) and therefore is tremendously limited in getting results. Not every country has our phobia about communism. The monster 'communism' has grown completely out of proportion in the U.S. It has taken on all sorts of shapes and meanings and causes us to do stupid things, like bankrolling Senegalese students to go to the States. A dangerous situation, which could bankrupt us further. Isn't Vietnam doing enough damage?

Because of this fanatic fear we have supported corrupt regimes and put our country in the position of being known as a "soft touch". At least I had a chance to say 'No' to a scam while my boss was away.

One day an Embassy officer rushed into my office and quickly closed the door behind him. Then in a hushed voice he told me that he had word that a young Dahomean was hiding out at the university and needed help. "He escaped from the Soviet Union and is afraid they are after him," the Embassy officer's tone was serious. "Can the Consulate give him enough money to get back to Dahomey?" he added as though our national security depended on it.

The usual CIA reaction would have been to send the stranded student a small amount of money and try to lure him into a meeting with promises of more money.

But, knowing University students pretty well by this time, my answer was. "Tell your contact to notify the young man hiding out at the University to send me his passport, showing his Soviet entry visa and I will help him." The Embassy officer, in favor of giving him money, was shocked and objected. But he understood my point when I told him that I had found out from my student friends that when things got dull at the University they would think up some wild story about the Soviets to tell the Americans. Not only was this fun, they sometimes got dollars for their "information".

The officer passed my message on to his University contact and we never heard another word from the "frightened student hiding out in the University."

(Thursday 9 November)

It seems almost unreal that a few months ago I didn't expect to be here in my nest. But I'm glad for the delay. I'm sitting at my desk, facing the open French doors. Beyond is the lush green of my back garden and the bright blue sky above. I have always known I could be happy here (even working long hours) with the right playmate. Even though it is a house without romantic memories, it is charming and in its own way has brought me happiness, but I want to live more fully. This is my first long experience of having absolutely no one—not even a pen pal. A few years ago such an experience would have destroyed me, but somehow I manage to bear this emptiness, perhaps because there is still hope, quiet and patient hope that comes with age.

I still don't have plans for my freedom. But then, freedom is being free of everything—even plans. I will do all the things I want to when the time is perfect for each thing. Skiing is the only activity that has to fit into certain time, everything else will come when the spirit moves me. I will probably leave here by ship and perhaps stop off in Morocco for a week or so and then to the Canary Islands before landing in Europe.

(Friday 10 November)

Jacqueline returned from France this morning looking rested and a few pounds heavier. She and her no-good husband came for lunch. I'd already told her that her blanket had been stolen. When I gave her one of my blankets I looked her husband straight in the eyes, but he didn't blink. Maybe he wasn't the thief, but I still suspect him. I had to drive them out to their little house in the Medina where he has been living since she's been away. I just as soon not see him again, but it hurts her feelings when I try to exclude him.

(Saturday 18 November)

From Monday through Friday I worked until midnight. Today was a glorious day; tennis and then breakfast on the N'Gor Hotel terrace with Pat. In my new skimpy bikini (good thing I'm thin or it wouldn't cover the necessary parts) I braved the choppy sea. Pat timidly joined me. There were few people on the beach. Lunch at the N'Gor and then we settled down on our mattress under an umbrella and slept. A swim afterwards revived us. Drinks with Luis and Milu and then a dinner party at Edmond's, a charming African who is the next Senegalese Ambassador to Yugoslavia. We danced the twist all evening. Thank goodness I've been practicing.

Last week I bought a Chubby Checkers record, came home and put it on the turntable in the study. I was gyrating, full speed ahead, when I whirled around and came face to face with Mamadou. He'd come to put away an armful of towels, but unable to suppress his laughter, he fled.

(Sunday 19 November)

This morning before I could plan a nice restful Sunday my gardener came, breaking my blessed silence and bringing frustration. I really didn't want to get involved, but he needed directions. Should I, or should I not, get rid of those large pots of dead ferns? I finally decided to throw them into the sea with hope of finding time to replace them with new life. Now the garden looks naked and I'm reminded, more than ever, that I must turn some attention to its beauty. I had grown accustomed to the scraggly plants in the old pots and my conscience had stopped bothering me. I will now have to replace them before next weekend. I've sent out Seventy five invitations to a buffet-cocktail dance party.

The day flew. Wind surfed with British friends, played tennis afterwards at their Embassy, and then danced the twist and cha-cha-cha with Charles Louis at Bounette's. I feel good vibes with him. He is very witty. Have I already lost perspective?

(Wednesday 22 November)

I shall never forget this day. I've had a toothache for the past two days and this morning I went to the French dentist. He said I'd have to have a root canal. I agreed to let him do it, but emphasized that he'd have to do so without Novocain because I couldn't stand having a needle stuck in my mouth. Not believing that I could go through with it, he prepared a shot of Novocain. I assured him I would be all right if he would tell me when the worst was over. As he worked I could see perspiration on his tense, thin, middle-aged face.

Each time the pain increased he would pause and ask if I wanted the needle. I'd shake my head. When he finally finished he wiped the sweat from his angry face and said in harsh, stinging French, "Please don't ever come to me again. I'm not accustomed to torturing my patients."

When I walked out of his office I was floating. Everything looked so clear, the trees a brilliant green, the sea breeze stimulated every nerve in my body and the sharp, clear, street noise seemed electrically amplified. Is prolonged, intense pain a drug?

(Sunday 26 November)

From the moment I awakened yesterday at 6:30 until this morning at 0100 hours I was in a spin. I had planned last night's party for seventy-five when I was in one of those rare, rested modes, but when the time came I was already exhausted from a week of hard work. Realizing what I'd done, I wanted to pull the covers over my head and hope it would all go away. Instead I jumped out of bed and didn't stop, except to have my hair done, during which I slept. In the afternoon Charles-Louis and his gang came over and moved all the furniture out of the living room to make space for dancing. Then they set up bars in the front and back gardens and decorated the apartment with Charles-Louis' paintings (abstract) and arm loads of flowers they had brought. At one point I realized they'd disappeared and went looking for them. I found them in my study pouring through a large art book on Hindu temple erotic sculpture. Their embarrassment embarrassed me. It was hard to believe that young Frenchmen would be embarrassed by pictures of art, but I must admit this art was extremely erotic.

I mistakenly thought that the more servants I hired to serve and take care of drinks, the easier it would be on me. Wrong! There was one panicky moment, after the Ambassador arrived, when I realized that no one had a drink. I couldn't leave my place at the garden gate. People were pouring in and I had to receive them. Some, house guests of Brits and Americans, I didn't even know. As for Africans, they usually bring their friends. There was masses of room, front and back gardens, enormous living-dining room, yet the guests congregated on the walkway behind me. Finally I caught Charles-Louis' eye and asked him to move some of the people to the back garden bar. The problem solved itself when the guests discovered the dining table, laden with food.

Although it was a cocktail-*dansant* from 6:30 to 8:30, it wasn't until 9:30 that the party thinned out to a comfortable forty people.

Some guests, including the Ambassador, had to go on to dinner parties. The African and French contingents were having such a good time dancing that they would have stayed until dawn, but at two O'clock I whispered to a British friend that I was exhausted and she broke up the party.

I awakened this morning to the sound of the doorbell, I thanked God that it was Sunday. I didn't even mind seeing my dressmaker. She is making the few shabby dresses, left behind by the thief, into charleston-skirted or hip-belted styles.

I feel sorry for her. She's pale and looks anemic. Her blond hair seems thinner each time I see her. Against her family's wishes she married an African she met at a French university. They were happy in France, but when he brought her back to his Moslem family they treated her like an outcast. After four years and two children her life was so miserable she left her husband and set up a tiny place for herself and children in the Medina. She said that neither her family nor his wanted the half-caste children. Luckily her mother taught her to sew when she was a teenager.

(Friday 1 December)

Two days ago we got word that my replacement had been named. She will arrive in February. Why don't I feel happy? Is it Charles-Louis?

At least I will get to see the west coast of Africa before I leave. An Air Attaché plane, on its way from Europe to Cape Town, South Africa, will stop here and Pat and I will take a diplomatic bag to Lome, Togo. From there we will make our own way to Dahomey and Nigeria. We have visas and return tickets.

(Saturday 2 December)

After working late all last week, I took off today and went to the beach. I didn't enjoy myself because I hadn't yet packed for the trip. I was about to give up my comfortable beach mattress and go home to pack, when I saw our Administrative Officer arrive with the Air Attaché and the plane's crew. They settled down at the outside bar. All the time they were having a drink I wondered what they were talking about. Somehow I sensed that the plane would go without us. If the verdict was "no" at least I could stay at the beach with my friends. The Admin Officer, who must have felt my eyes on him, looked my way and immediately came over and gave me the bad news. There were no seats available, too much cargo, also they didn't want to take women.

Charles-Louis, Bounette and Alain came home with me for drinks and wanted me to go to Gorée Island with them, but I declined. I'm trying to resist seeing them so often even though they make me laugh and feel young again. They are so carefree. Charles Louis is here in Dakar doing his military service. So far he seems to have spent most of his time painting portraits of the top Army Officers and their wives. One weekend, soon after he arrived here, he forgot to return to barracks and was arrested and thrown into the brig for going AWOL, but it didn't interrupt his painting a portrait of the Commanding Officer and his wife. Each day the MPs marched him from the brig to the General's residence and stood guard while he worked on the portraits then marched him back to jail. It didn't bother him, his spirit of freedom can't be fenced in. On the contrary it gave him funny stories to tell. He's good at acting out his stories and keeps us in stitches. I love to laugh. I used to say that someday I would marry a clown, but I've found out that clowns are often sad people in real life.

(Wednesday 6 December)

I'm retiring my movie camera. Today when Queen Elizabeth passed Independence Square on the way to the Presidential Palace, I was in place on the curb. I saw her coming, sitting regally in an open car dressed in pale blue, smiling and waving. I put the camera to my eye and watched her approach and then

zap she was gone. I didn't really see her and yet she passed almost within reach. I wanted to look into her eyes and smile at her. Alas!

Now that my replacement has been named, the wheels are turning. Headquarters are now preparing to ship my household effects back to the States. There are moments when I dread cutting off my relations with the Government. I know I'm going to miss all the privileges. I'm also going to miss my excellent cook (the Ambassador's wife wants him) and my active life here, but the coming year of freedom holds promise of adventure.

(Friday 8 December)

I've declared Saturdays and Sundays days of silence during which I want to think of my friends and family and send them Christmas and New Year's wishes. Charles—Louis has made charming cards for me; sketches of Africans in various costumes made from swatches of local, bright-colored material. He is so clever.

In Magda's Christmas card she said, "Ernst got married to a lovely woman named Elizabeth. She's very much like you. Are you surprised?" Of course not! Apparently he found a strong, stable woman who was willing (as I wasn't) to be the anchor in a marriage. He's a perfect companion, well brought up, highly educated, artistic, speaks five languages, etc., but too unstable to take on family responsibilities. Perhaps he has settled down in the past year. I wish him all the happiness he gave me. Through him I discovered India.

(Saturday 9 December)

Charles-Louis and I took a picnic to a deserted beach late this afternoon. We swam, ran on the beach, explored the bush bordering the white sand, pretending we'd been shipwrecked on an uninhabited island. In general, behaved like children. For the first time in ages I felt free. The world melted away. We drank wine and ate cold lobster and mangoes until the sunset faded. Then we lay on the beach and watched the stars appear as the sky blackened. I've finally given in to the inevitable.

(Tuesday 26 December)

I've neglected my diary for over two weeks. So many unrecorded emotions, some too personal to record.

About a week ago I had an unexpected house guest, secretary (one of "us") from Bamako, so clandestine meetings with Charles-Louis had to be at odd moments. Sometimes late at night. She finally had the good taste to move to the hotel.

Christmas made me aware of how much I'm going to miss my good friends here. On Christmas eve I took Luis and Milu a Charles-Luis' painting, for a Christmas present, and they insisted I stay. They were lonely, so I waited until almost time for midnight mass then shared their pleasure watching their seven-year-old son, Andres, open his presents. Many years have passed since I had the pleasure of sharing Christmas with children.

Later as I walked across the street to my house the sidewalks were filled with people on their way to midnight mass. I remembered Christmases of my childhood and felt lonely. Later I had a short outburst of tears while wrapping presents. I tied a ribbon on the last gift at two o'clock.

Christmas morning I readied the house for an evening party. I kept being interrupted by public workers, postman, policeman, street cleaner, etc. coming for their presents. Finally I found a tennis partner and vented my emotions hitting tennis balls. In the afternoon I took presents to my boss and his family. They gave me a lovely bottle of Channel and a leather-bound edition of Voltaire's *Candide*. Jacqueline and husband came by for a drink. I wasn't even embarrassed to give her a present, but nothing for him. From 6:30 to 7:30 I went to open house at the Ambassador's residence. Then to Luis and Milu for a traditional Portuguese Christmas dinner. Just the three of us and Andrés.

After Andres' nanny came we gathered up trays of food and went across to my house to prepare a midnight buffet. It was great fun. About twenty people arrived at ten o'clock, including Charles-Louis, Bounette and Alain. Half of the guests were Luis and Milu's friends. At midnight we gathered around the buffet table featuring a whole, roasted suckling pig, which we'd had fun decorating. Everyone left at 2:30. Charles-Louis came back to wish me a special Christmas and tell me how much fun we would have in Paris. He leaves in January to attend the *Haute Ecole des Arts Decoratif*. He was one of thirty chosen out of eight hundred.

(Saturday 31 December)

This past week is a blur. I went to two parties and worked every night the rest of the week. And now I'm faced with a New Year's Eve party. But it will be easy and informal; just Luis and Milu, Charles-Louis, his gang and some of their friends. They are bringing food and drink. I'd much rather prepare the party on my own, otherwise it's disorganized. But organization is not a necessity for my artist friends. They're happier without its confines. Heaven only knows what it will be like. I don't even know half of the people they're bringing. When I look back over my diary I see that I have spent a lot of time either giving or attending dinner parties. Entertaining is the major pastime here, as it was in Turkey, Iran and India. It's always enjoyable if the guests are interesting, and so easy with servants to do all the work, and affordable with duty-free wine and whiskey. Seeing the New Year in this year was a special pleasure, surrounded by friends, most of whom I will soon leave forever.

PART III

1962

(Monday 1 January)

Slept off my hangover on the beach after a slugging game of tennis. Went home with plans to get a good night's sleep, but soon after I had a bath Charles-Louis, Bounette and a couple other French friends dropped by to thank me for a good time last night and before I knew it we were having another party. There was a feast of leftovers and wine.

When Bounette and I were putting out the food she intimated that she knew Charles-Louis was secretly seeing me. I blushed even though she is all in favor.

I received a book on Japan for Christmas which turned my thoughts back to those happy days with Norman. That exotic country was a perfect setting for a magic romance.

(Saturday 6 January)

We are undergoing a crisis at work and I've been at the office twelve hours a day. I haven't even had time to hand in my formal resignation, much less make travel plans. I'm not eager to leave Dakar. I'm never anxious to leave a post. Either I've just met someone I hate to leave behind or I've been seeing someone for a year or so and am in love. Also I hate making changes, leaving behind friends, pulling up roots, going to a new country with my life in packing cases, making friends and a place for myself and working for a new boss, who might not like me. I get panicky just thinking of it. But the bell rings and it's time to move on. Ready or not.

Meanwhile, if I'm to finish everything I will have to work at least twelve hours a day. It is a job for two people and I'm afraid when my replacement arrives she will not even attempt to do it alone.

(Monday 8 January)

Farewell parties for Charles-Louis are in full swing. I've met lots of new French people. They are fun loving as well as good conversationalists. We eat, drink wine and cha-cha-cha, or twist, until the wee hours. No one in my group ever drinks too much. They don't need to as they are always upbeat.

(Tuesday 9 January)

Last night I went to the Ambassador's reception for the Golden Gate Quartet, which is here to give two performances. I knew many of the guests, Africans and foreign diplomats, but I hadn't met two handsome French movie stars making a film here. Now that I know a lot of people I'm not so shy about speaking French. The Quartet gave a performance that was sufficient for me, but the Ambassador asked each of us to attend the two public performances and take a couple of African guests with us. I dare say that I will be the only American to do this, except the higher diplomats (Men) who will get free tickets.

After the reception I went to dinner at Bounette's apartment. It was a small farewell party for Charles-Louis. He was supposed to leave at 4:00 a.m., but at 0300 hours word came by phone that the plane from South Africa to Paris was not coming. He would have to wait another day. I immediately said, "Good! Another farewell party at my house tomorrow night."

It's just as well that he is leaving. I can't cope with seeing him and working twelve hours a day. We both look forward to meeting again in Paris. He already has a small apartment-cum-studio on the Ile de St. Louis, where there will be no prying eyes. I will be free to be me, whatever form that takes.

(Wednesday 10 January)

Today (Charles-Louis' last day) was hectic. Joan, who was sent out, on temporary duty, to help me get caught up on my work, arrived at 3:00 a.m. No one was there to meet her. We didn't receive the telegram announcing her arrival. So she found her way into Dakar and sat in the hotel lobby until the Embassy opened. I had to rescue her and find a hotel. None available. I settled her in an empty Embassy apartment. I couldn't have her stay with me at this traumatic time in my life. I wasn't even able to take the day off to be with Charles-Louis, but we had a couple of hours on the beach after lunch. It's a shame that finally I've found someone to have fun with, but don't have time to spend with him.

By the time I took Joan out to dinner and back to the apartment where she is staying I barely had time to get properly dressed for Charles-Louis last farewell party. I invited only a few of his closest friends. Mamadou made us a cold buffet of lobster, shrimp, ham, various cold salads, cheese, fruit and wine. The party lasted from ten o'clock until long after midnight, during which there were some tremendous, heated discussions about art, which I couldn't always follow. We took Charles-Louis to his plane at 3:30 a.m. and by the time I got home and into bed it was almost five o'clock.

(Thursday 11 January)

I had planned to spend my lunch hour sleeping, but Joan didn't want to eat alone so I asked her to lunch with me, thus giving away my only chance to rest. In the evening I took some African friends to see and hear the Golden Gate Quartet. I had to work until the last moment with no time to eat dinner, much less rest. Again it was midnight when I fell into bed. This is hard on me. I need eight hours of sleep each night.

(Friday 12 January)

Kathleen, my Irish friend who makes me laugh, came to lunch. She said she knew about Charles-Louis. "I saw it in your eyes and sensed the electricity between you two the day he came to collect his paintings." She is a few years my senior, unmarried and mature in her views of human relationships, which we discussed at length.

I felt obligated to ask Joan to dinner. She looked so lost. While we were having before-dinner drinks Alain, one of our French group who has become a close friend since Charles Louis left, dropped in. He looked forlorn. He is in love with a girl who is giving him a hard time so I asked him to stay for dinner.

(Saturday 13 January)

This morning I played tennis (exercise saves my sanity, gets rid of frustration and energizes me) then worked until one o'clock. I had planned to have a quiet lunch and rest, but an Agency visitor insisted on taking me to lunch. He wanted to discuss "business" with me. We drove out to the N'Gor Hotel, had a delicious lunch and good conversation. He was a complete stranger and I wondered what on earth we would talk about, but as he was from our Paris Station and interested in arts we had plenty in common. He had to be back at the office at three so I decided I might as well work the rest of the afternoon. I left the office at eight, rushed home, dressed, and went to dinner at Kathleen's apartment. Her keen Irish wit keeps me laughing. I shall never forget her story about flying out to her post in Turkey.

The plane had stopped in Athens for refueling. After it took off for Turkey and was a few miles out over the ocean the Captain announced that there was engine trouble and the plane would have to turn back. He ordered the passengers to put on life jackets and gave instructions on how to use them. Kathleen, thinking "this is it", said her rosary, then not wanting to ruin her new, expensive white-kid gloves carefully removed them and safely stored them in her coat pocket. All she could think of during those tense moments, which might have been her last, was, "What a pity! This would make such a terrific cocktail party story."

(Sunday 14 January)

I'm torn between staying home and making a packing list, writing a letter to Charles-Louis in French (a difficult task), or keeping my promise to go to the market with Bounette this morning and to the beach this afternoon. The sky is overcast, but the sun will come out and I'll want to go to the beach. I hate making decisions so I'll do all four things.

Thanks to Bounette and Charles-Louis my life for the past two months has been happy. Bounette came to work in the Embassy during the absence of our French receptionist. I immediately noticed something special about her. She had an exotic foreign-looking face, broad with high cheekbones, and olive skin and dark almond-shaped eyes. She was extremely polite, especially to me. She told me later that she could see another person underneath my cold efficient facade and knew we could be friends. One day I asked her to lunch because I heard that she was a sculptress. The moment we were away from the Embassy we started discovering one another.

She was born in Morocco, about 29 years ago. Her mother was from an old aristocratic French family and her father a glamorous, but completely unstable Moroccan artist. The marriage didn't last. She was sent to France to live with her maternal grandmother in an old chateau in the middle of a forest. There she led a lonely and unloved existence, seeing her grandmother only at meal times and the rest of the time being bullied by her governess. Finally when she was 16, awkward and physically unattractive, as she described herself, her mother, beautiful and gracious, sent her to a boarding school in England. Being the untamed animal that she was, having grown up in the mystery of the forest, she could not conform to the school and finally ran away and at the age of 17 started earning her own living. She entered the London art school and lived in poverty. Although she suffered from the lack of material necessities she was happy, even doing the washing-up in a night club to earn enough money to go to school. Her mother refused to help her after she left the boarding school. Being completely ignorant of conniving human beings she got involved with a bohemian group and was finally taken over and dominated by a Russian refugee, twenty years older, who made her life miserable. She was so terrified of him that she didn't have the courage to run away. Each time she tried, he threatened to kill himself. Finally she became desperate and took an overdose of sleeping pills. She was found and saved, but then she was taken to court because attempting suicide is a crime against the laws of England. In the end she was let go because she was so young.

She had always wanted to go to America, because it was a country of freedom from all the Old World restrictions. She got a chance to work as a governess to a rich American family. Her first year in the States was disappointing and miserable. She was tied financially to a family that turned her into a servant, but luckily her background was evident to people who frequented the family with whom she lived. One of the sympathetic families liberated her and helped her to continue her studies. Again she lived in poverty, but was happy doing her sculpture and all sorts of odd jobs to earn a living. But after four years, this sort of life began taking its toll and she became too exhausted and sick to continue. Meanwhile her mother married a Frenchman, below her socially, and came to live in Dakar. She asked Bounette to come and help in her children's nursery for which she would pay Bounette well. Bounette came, but since her mother had a bigger heart than a business sense (taking in poor children) she couldn't afford to pay Bounette.

Her hopes of earning and saving enough money to sculpt in peace and quiet, without starving to death, have faded. She is trapped into living in a small flat with her mother and step father. She doesn't even have the privacy of her own room, much less a place to work. In desperation, she gave up sculpture and learned to type in order to earn a living. She is completely unsuited for a desk job.

Contrasting my life with hers is interesting. I have served my term in the confinement of "earning a living" and am now being liberated, a much wiser person with a clear conscious that I have paid my debt. I'm now free to create, if I have the ability, in comparatively comfortable surroundings and without worry of where I'll get my next meal. For me this was a much better cycle. When I was young I was too immature and restricted by social structure. Bounette is going through the same thing as Magda. How they succeed, faced with material realism, remains to be seen. Magda, who used to be contemptuous of me because I couldn't share my life between the working world and the creative world, is now finding out how difficult it is.

Charles-Louis, on the other hand, is both a painter and a normal, well-balanced individual. He is young but self— disciplined in his work. He was born in Indochina where his father was working for the French Colonial Government. He lived most of his life outside France. He had two years of art study in Paris before having to do his military service. Luckily he was allowed to serve here where he could afford a studio. I met him through Bounette and from the beginning thought him charming and amusing, but never dreamed that I would be emotional involved with him. In spite of the difference in our ages, we were good for one another.

For him I opened a door to an entirely different life style. He loved my stories of adventures in the countries where I had lived, especially India. Through his attention and affection he made me feel alive and happy again. Sometimes even attractive. Everyone noticed a change in me. I had become almost human, proving there is still a lot of life and laughter left inside me. I'm ready now, more than ever, to begin the next chapter of my life. One thing about the French. They are not as sensitive to age as Americans are. "Good friends are all the same age," Charles-Louis used to say. We shall see when we meet in Paris.

(Tuesday 16 January)

I was invited to the grand opening of the new Plaza Cinema. President Senghor, his cabinet and foreign diplomats will be there. When opening a cinema warrants the attendance of the country's leaders and the diplomatic corps I realize how provincial this capital city really is.

(Monday 21 January)

Charles-Louis' letters, full of word pictures of Paris, make me more and more eager to join him. My doubts about his not wanting to see me there were unfounded. He has already contacted Nena, my American friend, and plans a big welcome party for me.

I suppose it's natural that I now feel close to my French friends, Bounette, Michelle and Alain because we all miss Charles-Louis. He was the bright light that drew us together.

Yesterday (Sunday)

Bounette and I were just about to have lunch at the N'Gor Beach restaurant when Michelle and Alain arrived. We spoke of Charles-Louis and wondered what he was doing. Soon more of Bounette's friends joined us and we got on the subject of nervous breakdowns and shock treatment as a cure. One of the women had just been through the treatment and described at length the

dreadful psychological effects. Bounette and most of her friends
were against such barbarism.

Bounette came home with me and soon the gang followed.
My house has become the Sunday evening literary salon.
Always interesting topics of conversation. Good for my French.
Luis and Milu arrived, followed by Michelle and Alain and
then later Alain "the bearded". He had a bad cold and was
exhausted after the German President's visit for which he was
the interpreter.

After everyone left Bounette and I ate cold chicken and
discussed marriage, of all things. Neither of us is interested in
making that commitment. Later Milu returned because she was
fed up listening to Luis and Antonio talking politics. She kept us
laughing. Soon Luis and Antonio arrived and Antonio, Portuguese,
short in stature, but handsome and very sexy, amused us for
another half-hour with stories of women in his life. By the time
they all left I felt miserable and this morning I'm unable to go to
the office. Something is wrong. I have a violent headache. But I
must try to go to the office.

(Thursday 25 January)

I'm going through disillusionment about my work. I think the
whole operation is useless. Our foreign policy toward West Africa
seems a huge waste of money, especially our aid programs. The
money is squandered. Senegal is France's responsibility, not ours.
I hate to feel this way because I might have to return to work and
it will be twice as difficult if I no longer believe in it.

A constant headache has plagued me for days. So rare. I've
had few headaches in my life. I was on weekend duty and worked
into the night. Milu and Luis feel neglected by me. They are
sensitive and jealous of my French friends. So I took time this
evening to go see them. Luis was sitting at the dining table working
on a pile of papers. He runs the entire Portuguese Consulate by
himself. He doesn't even have a secretary. Milu and I read our

horoscopes from a French women's magazine and about midnight we took a drive, in my car (he doesn't have one), around the corniche, to gaze at the full moon's path across the water.

(Friday 26 January)

This morning the Ambassador informed me that he'd received a letter from my replacement saying that she was coming out by ship. That's the limit! It will take weeks. Yesterday a letter from Jo Thompson's friend, Liz Harter, invited me to stop off in Casablanca and stay a week or so. How kind of her. She doesn't really know me, but we work for the same organization.

This is Joan's last day. She has helped me, but there is still more to be done. As I told my boss, this is a job for two women. The code work alone is one job. One other person is needed to handle deep-cover agents, write up their reports, do all the administrative, clerical and financial work. Tonight she wants to take me out to dinner to show her appreciation for my attention. I don't really want to go. After a large meal with wine it will be difficult to return to the office and finish encoding messages. Also I will have to get up at 0230 to take her to the airport to catch her plane to Paris.

(Saturday 27 January)

I had to stay at the airport with Joan until her plane finally left at 0530 hours because she doesn't speak French and I didn't want to leave her alone. I got back in bed and was soon shivering with cold under only one blanket. I once had three blankets. I gave one to Jacqueline and loaned one to Joan. She left it at the apartment and I'll have to go tomorrow and fetch it.

Still no word on my replacement's arrival date. And no departure date or travel arrangements for me.

(Friday 26 January)

Peace is with me. I'm too exhausted to struggle and, more important, the end is in sight. It's too good to be true. Soon I'll be waking up to days to be filled with what I **want** to do and not what I **must** do. I'm afraid to hope too much for fear of casting the evil eye on the bright spot awaiting me.

(Saturday 27 January)

Worked in the morning. Played tennis with Lois in the afternoon. Refused Jacqueline's invitation to tea. Dinner with Ruth.

(Sunday 28 January)

I've been listening to Bach's B Minor Mass this morning, while waiting for potatoes to boil. We are going on a picnic and I'm making the potato salad. I'm not very enthusiastic, but once I hear Bounette's voice calling, "Lizabet" and the garden gate closes behind me I will come alive and the day will happily unfold.

We, Bounette, Alain and Michelle, Alain the Second and his companion, Madu, and heaven only knows who else Bounette has found along the way, are going to M'Bour for the day. Bounette claims the sun is brighter and the sea warmer there. We shall find out. Whatever, it will not be the same without Charles—Louis.

(Two hours later).

Still no Bounette. The potatoes finished boiling. I made salad. Not enough potatoes. I boiled more and added them to the salad. Now there're too many potatoes and I've run out of mayonnaise. Oh, well, at least I'll escape the kitchen, with a sink full of dirty dishes and potatoes skins, have another cup of coffee and talk to my diary until Bounette comes.

(Sunday Night)

I'd just lit a cigarette when Bounette appeared at my garden gate followed by Alain, who looked ten years younger and very handsome after shaving off his beard. I felt embarrassed being so intimate, kisses on both cheeks, with a face I wasn't accustomed to. A sensitive face with a dimpled chin.

We gathered beach umbrellas, ice bucket, roast chickens and potato salad and climbed into Alain-the-Second's big car. We were off! Two hours late and only five adventurers. The others decided at the last moment that they couldn't go. *Tant pis!*

It was a beautiful day, warm and windy. The countryside, although brown and dry, showed signs of spring with new life. Where there was water, the fields were green with vegetables, otherwise barren fields were covered with squash, like great round, green objects of all sizes scattered on the parched earth as though a jolly giant had strewn them there.

When we reached M'Bour, Bounette wanted to visit the bird market (*Marche des oiseaux*). Unfortunately we never found the birds, but we didn't leave the market place until B. had examined, touched and smelled almost everything in the place. She caused great amusement by trying on and then buying an African wig and before we left she persuaded me to buy one too, which she claimed would make a sensational evening coiffeur. "If you can't use it, you can make it into a collage," she said. We found some wonderful little primitive clay animals; a laughing cow and a chicken with elephant-sized feet and a sad expression on its face. But unfortunately the merchant wouldn't lower his price and to save face we didn't buy the animals. Pity!

Bounette was right. The sun was brighter and the water warmer. We unloaded umbrellas, hampers of food, and bottles of wine on the deserted beach. Before launching into a tasty meal we had a swim in the comforting emerald-green sea. After lunch Michelle, Alain S. and I slept in the sun while Bounette and Alain-the-Second gathered objects for a collage. They returned with bits of colored glass, sea fans, bones, dried fish skin, sponge, driftwood and even a bright blue shirt collar (abandoned in fit of passion?). Jointly we made a strange collage in the sand. Another swim, more chicken and camembert and another bottle of wine. Soon the day ended in long shadows and a cool breeze which brought out sweaters (Alain had an extra one for me). Reluctantly we packed up and left, saying, What a wonderful day it has been. "But how much better," someone added, "If Charles-Louis had been with us."

On the way back to Dakar we came across a crowd of people just outside M'Bour village. We stopped to see what was going on, expecting to find Sunday afternoon *Lutte* (wrestling). Instead we found horse racing in an open field. Bounette and I got excited and wanted to stay for the last two races. What a wonderful experience; hundreds of Africans (no Europeans) all dressed in their best khaftan-like boubous, milling about in the dust, talking and laughing in loud voices, making bets among themselves and seemingly having a good time. The horses were being paraded. Most of them suffering from some sort of a wound, some already exhausted from having run in the last race and a peculiar long-legged one with back legs longer than the front ones. It looked more like a camel than a horse. The horses were covered in plastic *gri-gris (blanket), to* which Bounette and I objected. We have nothing against *gri-gris*, but plastic *gri-gris*. Ugh! The jockeys wore everything from the latest jockey fashions in colored silk to bright sport shirts and baggy trousers. Some were barefooted, some were wearing American cowboy boots, and some were in their stockings. All were extremely thin and, as Africans can be at times, very tall. As I watched them get lined up for the takeoff, I felt as though I were watching a comic 1930's movie to the tune of tom-toms.

THEY WERE OFF! The jockey's arms and legs flying in all

directions, their body tilted back and completely unbalanced, each beating his horse with a long whip while at the same time pulling back on the reins as they shot forward down the sandy field. There were obviously no horse lovers in the audience, otherwise they would have been outraged by such treatment. They, horses and riders out of control, galloped around the improvised sand track, which in itself must have been hard on the horse's hoofs. We could only see the tops of their heads as they zoomed past, because we were behind a ten-deep band of onlookers.

Here in Africa there is not even that basic peasant politeness toward "guests", which I've always found in countries where I've lived. (But then the French are no longer guests, they are 'colons'.) We were pushed further into the background and saw little of the last race.

The winner was an eleven-year-old boy who looked no more that seven. He was given a tom-tom ovation and led away by his admirers.

We were about to leave when suddenly a sea of hostile black faces, led by two tom-tom players, confronted us. Standing face to face with Bounette, the drummers, hate in their eyes, started beating out their war cry. The crowd grew larger. Bounette stood her ground and we backed her up (my heart pounding with fear, having experienced the danger of hostile crowds in Tehran). Our eyes met theirs and within minutes, which seemed hours, we knew that we had won, and the scene ended as suddenly as it had begun.

The auto route was filled with cars of all descriptions. Before arriving at Rusfisque we saw a terrible accident; a *car rapide* turned over in the middle of the road, strewn with glass, bloody patches and three smashed cars on the roadside. The injured had already been taken away. I knew that this was a regular Sunday occurrence, but it was still horrifying when one comes face to face with it.

When we arrived in Dakar we stopped to buy bread for dinner and cigarettes for Bounette at a little *epicerie,* in front of Charles

Louis' former storefront studio. It was dark and empty and shrouded in memories for each of us. The trees in front had not escaped the recent tree-chopping mania, spreading through Dakar like a tidal wave. They have cut down all the old trees in Place Protet, leaving it naked and ugly. The Senegalese call it progress.

Our perfect day ended with gin and tonic, left over chicken, camembert and wine and a heated discussion on religion, everybody against Bounette, an atheist, as usual. Milu came, leaving Louis at home discussing politics with Antonio (one of Luis' secret agents).

(Monday 29 January)

British Embassy Reception for officers on Canadian ships at six. Visited Milu for few minutes afterwards. Worked from nine to midnight.

(Tuesday 30 January)

Cocktail party aboard Canadian ship. Stayed afterwards for party in Officers' Lounge. Home at 0100 hours.

(Wednesday 31 January)

Jacqueline came for lunch. Worked until midnight.

(Thursday 1 February)

Dinner with Regine, a French artist friend, who is preparing an art exhibit.

(Friday 2 February)

Bounette came to dinner. We exchanged notes on Charles-Louis' activities in Paris. He's waiting to receive me.

(Saturday 3 February)

Worked all morning. Played tennis with Ruth. Went to fetch Regine and Bounette for art exhibit of Dutch painter. Sporting club for drinks afterwards with Alain. Dinner at my house. French Navy dance. Got home at 0430.

(Sunday 4 February)

Slept until 0900 hours. Headache. Gardener came. Letters to Charles-Louis and Liz in Casablanca. Took letters to airport post office. Picked up Jacqueline for my Sunday Salon (open house) for twelve. Ended at midnight.

(Monday 5 February)

Worked until midnight.

(Tuesday 6 February)

Stayed home in morning. Played tennis with Boss's wife. Had dinner with Kathleen.

(Wednesday 7 February)

Dinner party for British friends recently posted to Dakar.

(Thursday 8 February)

Bounette came to lunch. Dinner for six guests.

(Friday 9 February)

A "visitor" (one of us) from our Paris Station came to lunch. A charming man, who promises to be a good contact in Pairs. Reception at University.

(Saturday 10 February)

I've almost finished my backlog at the office. One more week of working at night and I should be ready to start turning my attention to my own problems, if there's not a crisis.

Today I slept until eight. Rare for me. Played tennis from nine to ten. By the time I got home and dressed it was almost eleven. On my way to work I met an African friend and we had a long conversation, mostly I was trying to explain why I'd neglected my African friends. They didn't fit in with my new French friends, but I didn't say so. I got to the office at 11:30, encoded telegrams until 1:00 p.m. Lunch at home. Dressmaker arrived at three. After a fitting, I returned to the office and worked until 8:00 p.m. I've just finished dinner and hope to be in bed by nine. So life goes on in the same old way as though it will never end and sometimes I don't think it will.

(Sunday 11 February)

Wrote letter to Charles-Louis. Visit from Ruth. Dressmaker, who is working hard to finish updating my dresses. Hand laundry. Beach from 11:30-5:30. Lunch at beach with Pat and Jean. Lovely drive back in cool evening. Prepared house for party. Wore new blue polka-dot silk evening slacks. Fifteen for dinner. It was a successful Sunday Salon. Ended at 1:00 a.m. I'm known among the Americans as the Pearl Mesta of Dakar.

(Monday 12 February)

Dentist, who agreed to pull a back tooth if I took Novocain. And then he extracted the tooth before the Novocain took effect. Very Painful! He sent an impression of my mouth to Paris to have a new bridge made. Meanwhile what if my teeth shift? Worked until 8:00 p.m. Visited Milu and Louis. I'm exhausted.

(Tuesday 13 February)

Bounette came to lunch. Drinks after lunch with Pat. Dinner with Bounette and her mother. Talked until after midnight. More exhausted.

(Wednesday 14 February)

Dressmaker at lunch time. Dentist. Bridge didn't fit. Another impression. By this time I felt as though I'd reached the end of my strength, which I thought was infinite, but I will not give up. The end is in sight. Half-hour rest. Etienne's (an artist friend of Bounette's) photo exhibit. Cocktails with British diplomat. Surprise party for Etienne. Home by eleven. Sick all night with upset stomach.

(Thursday 15 February)

I was still sick, but dragged myself to the office. As hard as I'd worked to finish the backlog, by one o'clock I had to give up—one day and a half before my replacement arrives on Saturday morning. I was too sick to eat lunch, in spite of Mamadou's urging. Slept most of afternoon. I'd invited some African friends to a "working" dinner for my boss and rather than try to call it off I went shopping at 6:30 for cheese and wine. Five guests arrived at eight. Halfway through dinner I had to go to bed. Stomach pains and nausea. My boss's wife took over.

(Friday 16 February)

Stayed in bed all morning. No appetite, exhausted, fever. Went to doctor at 11:30. Couldn't stay. Too sick. Canceled luncheon date with Kathleen. Doctor came in afternoon. Signs of jaundice. Louis' friend, Edmond, came to see about me.

(Saturday 17 February)

Still in bed. Went for urine test. Missed cocktail party aboard British ship. Friends came. I'm reading *The Leopard.*

(Sunday 18 February)

My eyes haven't turned yellow. The doctor is not sure if I have jaundice. Friends came. My replacement, Anne arrived on the plane from Pairs at 4:30 a.m. this morning. After resting all day she came to see me. Finding me in bed with an undiagnosed illness made her uneasy. She already is disillusioned in Dakar. Reading: *To Kill A Mockingbird.*

(Monday 19 February)

Still in bed. Doctor decided to have blood tests made. My boss took me to hospital. After brutalizing my poor arm for half an hour, trying to get a needle into the tiny vein, they put me on an operating table in case I fainted. After trying both arms, striking nerves on the way, they had to give up and let me rest. Finally the nurse called a specialist, who tried and failed. He then tried the veins in my hands. Further torture, but they got enough blood for the test. Actually I have been sick for the past month, but I have pushed myself, knowing that it would soon be over and I would be free. Friends came. Missed the British Embassy reception for ship's officers.

(Tuesday 20 February)

I finally got to the dentist. This time the bridge didn't fit much better, but I accepted it with a promise that I would have it remade in Paris. Went to the office in the afternoon. Worked until 7:00 p.m. Went to opening of Regine's art exhibit. A half-hour into the party I collapsed. Friends drove me home and put me to bed.

(Wednesday 21 February)

My blood test baffled the doctor. It showed something wrong with my liver, but I'm so tan he couldn't tell if my skin was yellow. He called in another doctor to take over the case. Meanwhile, I'm flat on my back, with no desire to eat or even to think of all the problems ahead. Tomorrow I hope to get the results and find out if I can leave next week.

(Thursday 22 February)

Last night I got sick again and spent the whole night in a cold sweat because I couldn't vomit. A French nurse, Bounette's friend, came to see me and said she believed there was something wrong with my bile and liver. Alain brought flowers.

I can barely hold my head up. I will not be able to leave next week. The first farewell party for me on Saturday has been canceled. My poor replacement is ready to resign. She says she can't do all the work. As usual I will be replaced by two people. It has happened at my last two posts. I, who haven't got a raise in seven years!

(Friday 23 February)

Another French doctor came. He said I had a *crise du foie (a liver attack)* and complete physical exhaustion. My blood pressure was dangerously low. My boss's wife had the doctor's prescription filled for me. I'm reading *"The Story of Philosophy"*.

(Saturday 24 February)

Started a ten-day series of shots. Still very weak. Missed outgoing pouch. Drove to airport to post letters to family. They must be worried. It's now 8:30 p.m. My last guest of the day has gone. Everyone thinks I'm snugly tucked into bed and carrying out the Doctor's orders. But here I am up to my old tricks of writing in my diary. Thank God my spirit is coming back. Although I hate feeling so physically helpless at least I'm beyond the struggle, which makes my fate easier to bear. For ten days I have been sick, most of the time in bed without thinking of all the things undone, my departure, etc. I have not even had the strength to be depressed or sorry for myself, which has been the greatest blessing. I have been reading and, recently, enjoying my friends' visits. After my ten-day treatment I have to remain in bed at least eight more days. I will not be able to leave on March second as planned. I will have to wait two more weeks for another ship. Whatever, it doesn't seem to really matter anymore. At least I will not have to spend the first month of my freedom getting my health back, as I did after I left India with amebic dysentery. And this time I will use some of my 1,000 hours of sick leave.

Spiritually speaking this illness has been disappointing. Usually my great illnesses (few that have been) are accompanied by introspective turmoil resulting in a discovery of myself, or sometimes a decision to change my life, as happened during my illness last year when I decided to suspend my career for as long as financially possible. Perhaps because this time there was no great pain involved. I find nothing so elucidating as the shock of extreme pain. This time my spirit seems as exhausted as my body, but a few more injections of science's latest life-giving fluids will kick-start my physical machine into action. At least I'm catching up on my reading, my favorite form of escapism. I've finished *To Kill a Mockingbird*, *The Leopard*, and *The Old Man and The Sea*. I was greatly moved by the film of The Old Man and expected to find an even greater message in the book, but like many things on which we build expectations, the reality was disappointing.

(Sunday 25 February)

In bed all day reading *The Story of Philosophy*. Bounette spent the evening with me.

(Monday 26 February)

After I went to the hospital for my daily injection I stopped by the library to get Machiavelli's famous book, *The Prince*. The Charge d'affaires wife came to see me.

(Tuesday 27 February)

My replacement, Anne, came to lunch. She is attractive,reserved, which makes her seem older than me. In the evening I went for a couple of hours to a surprise party for Regine after her art exhibit closed. I took Anne along to meet my friends. I could sense that they are not her type. I'm not surprised. Luis and Milu were there and almost ignored me. What's wrong?

My blood pressure has risen a bit and the doctor said I could go to the office two or three hours a week.

(Friday 2 March)

Well, you can imagine how that turned out. Wednesday I went in for three hours. Thursday for four hours and today I was at the office all day.(Stupid!) It was diplomatic pouch day and my poor replacement was near hysterics. I couldn't leave her in the lurch. She hasn't yet built up the speed I had attained. More than that, she doesn't want to work any overtime, even though I've told her it's a ten-hour-a-day job, plus Saturday mornings. My boss has already requested a code clerk, which will relieve her of half the workload. I keep promising to follow the doctor's orders to work only part time, but I can see now that it will be hard to do. My sense of duty to my job is much too strong. Either I work full time, or leave it completely alone. I can't do things halfway. I am my own worst enemy.

(Saturday 3 March)

Last night as I listened to the sea, pound against the rocks, I reckoned my illness had been a stroke of good luck. If I hadn't collapsed I would now be on the high seas and violently seasick on top of being completely exhausted. Also, if I hadn't collapsed I would have worked until the last minute, furthering my exhaustion. What a disaster that would have been, arriving in Casablanca a basket case for poor Liz to cope with. Now when I board the ship I will be in pretty good condition. The doctor said I couldn't ski right away. I must first adjust to the cold weather.

(Sunday 4 March)

I didn't expect my usual Sunday evening guests, because I have been sick for the past three weeks, but most of them came even before I'd had a shower. They thought it was my last week. They didn't stay long. I invited them to come next Sunday, my last open house.

My guests left and I have just finished washing the N'Gor Beach sand from my hair and sunburned body. It was one of those hot, sunny, but windy days, which is not always very pleasant, but I was happy because it was my first day at the beach since I fell ill. The doctor said I could lie in the sun, but not to go near the water. Pity! But I don't mind. I'm so glad to be almost well again, even though I won't be able to play tennis again before I leave.

On 16 March I will board the *Lyautey* for Casablanca. Now that I'm feeling better I'm beginning to get excited about my new adventure. In spite of the beautiful weather and my comfortable way of life my thoughts are already turning toward Paris and my year of freedom. I shall miss Bounette. Since I've been ill she has come to see me twice a day, at lunch and when she finishes work. Like Charles Louis (from whom I received a letter today) her actions and reactions are spontaneous. Her enthusiasm for life, childlike wonder, her fiery spirit and joyful laugh are so much like I remember Charles Louis.

My ship will arrive in Casablanca about March 20th. Liz will be there to meet me. She has a wonderful automobile tour of Morocco planned for us.

(Wednesday 7 March)

Today I get my last shot and another examination. The doctor said a little social life would be good for me (so French!), so I've been out two nights. One for a bridal shower for a girl in the Embassy and on Saturday night I went with Alain to a dinner-dance at the Navy Club. I was the only non-French guest.

(Thursday 8 March)

The doctor said I had made a miraculous recovery. My blood pressure is back to normal and my liver seems to be functioning again. Although I'm feeling much better I have developed a rash on the back of my neck, caused by a microbe in my nervous system, so the French doctor said. He gave me the hot iron treatment, i.e. he pressed a very hot flat iron, without a heat control, on the rash for only a second, killing the microbe and burning off a layer of skin. What a shock I got! I had no idea what he was going to do. Now I have an ugly, painful burn just where my collar rubs it raw. I try to keep it bandaged most of the time, but it will heal better, the doctor said, if I keep it exposed to the air. Wonder if he learned this barbaric practice from an African witch doctor.

(Sunday 11 March)

Friday the rash broke out on my face, just left of my mouth. Having coped with a fierce burn on the back of my neck, which is still raw, I told the doctor I didn't want that to happen to my face. He said I had no choice if I wanted to stop the rash from spreading to other parts of my body. Frightened, I reluctantly let him burn the rash. And now I've got this ugly great sore on my face. I have to leave it uncovered so it will heal quicker. What a way to bid good-bye to my friends. Because of it, I almost canceled my last Sunday Salon today, but as Bounette said, "Your friends would be hurt to think that your vanity meant more than friendship." She was right. I had the party and it was a great success. Mamadou outdid himself in laying out a cold supper. Oh, how I will miss him!

(Monday 12 March)

The weather is heavenly, which makes me dread the cold of Europe, especially since it means stockings for the first time in nineteen months. But then there is always spring in Paris.

My boss gave me a really posh farewell party. He invited all my friends, about sixty, including Embassy personnel. It was a great mixture of American, French, British, African and a few stray nationalities. Standing in the receiving line and watching the eyes of my guests as I greeted them was revealing. The vain and pretty and the unsure-of-themselves guests were uncomfortable and kept their eyes averted from the ugly place on my face. Whereas others like Bounette and her friends, sure of themselves, without vanity, let their eyes boldly explore my face. The party lasted until the wee hours. I couldn't resist dancing the twist, which exhausted me and I had to escape several times to my bedroom for a rest.

Saying *adieu* to Mamadou will be difficult. I will miss him almost as much as I'll miss my friends. He took good care of me. Anne plans to move into my house and employ him, but he told me he was thinking about returning to his tribe in *Haute Volta*.

(Friday 16 March) *AT SEA.* . . .

This evening at sunset I boarded the *Lyautey* for Casablanca. The last days are a jumble in my mind. Through a blur of tears I said good-bye to Mamadou, looked at my house for the last time, turned and entered an Embassy car, which took me to the harbor. The chauffeur said he would miss me. I had been kind to his family. I went early to the ship to see that arrangements had been made for a shipboard farewell party I was hostessing.

Soon the guests began to arrive, many carrying flowers. We drank champagne, ate *pâté foie gras*, reminisced, shed tears, embraced, kissed on cheeks and soon the Captain's voice came over the P.A. system: "All visitors ashore!"

With tears and brave smiles we embraced and said good bye, knowing we would never see one another again.

I was too emotional to stay on deck as the ship sailed away from the dock, leaving behind my friends waving and blowing kisses. I gave one last wave, went to my cabin, had a good cry and braced myself for the last look at Senegal.

As it receded into the darkness I dropped, one by one, the flowers from my friends into the sea, in which I'd learned to swim without fear and on whose shore I had spent many happy hours. As the last rose fell from my hand I looked up at the stars and my thoughts turned to Paris and a whole year of freedom to be ME.

END

EPILOGUE

After a month in Casablanca with Liz I regained my health and when I landed in Marseilles I was ready to ski in the French Alps. There, on the ski slopes in Megeve, I met Charles-Louis. The first month in Paris I stayed with my childhood friend, Nena, who showed me the Paris of fine dining and *haute couture* fashion shows (Dior, Balmain, Chanel). To enhance my freedom I bought a little British sports car convertible, which allowed me to move about Paris, to dance until dawn with Charles-Louis and his friends then drive home to Nena through the Bois de Boulogne with the top down and my scarf blowing in the wind. It was fun, but I wanted more.

After driving to Rome and back with Charles-Louis, I enrolled in the Sorbonne's Course in French Civilization (*Cours de Civilisation Francaise*) and moved to a little hotel on the Ile de la Cité. But I was still spending too much time on frivolous activities. Being frivolous was not the ME I was looking for, so I moved to a suite of rooms in a large apartment belonging to a French General's wife. Within walking distance of the Sorbonne I began my serious studying. Little by little I dropped out of Charles-Louis' artist group and made more mature French friends, who liked the theater, opera and ballet.

My year was soon over. I returned to the U.S.,crossing the Atlantic on the *SS Ile de la France*, and after a few months applied for my old CIA job. I was accepted at a higher salary, but I had to be reinvestigated to make sure that I hadn't been doing anything subversive during my absence.

At the end of my second year of freedom I rejoined the CIA. From June 1964 to June 1967 I was posted to Bogota, Colombia. Before leaving Colombia I bought a coffee farm in the Sierra Nevada mountains and left a caretaker in charge while I went off to serve a second two-year tour at the American Embassy in Tehran, Iran. In 1969 I returned to Headquarters in Washington, D. C. and retired at the end of that year, age 46.

I bought an apartment in Fort Lauderdale, but I couldn't settle down. I traveled to England, East Africa, Morocco, Russia and skied in the Austrian Alps. I wrote short stories and a novel and spent time at my coffee farm off and on until it became too dangerous to live there alone. In 1974 I reluctantly sold the farm to a young American couple, who wanted to get into the import-export business (drugs?). I later learned that they abandoned the farm.

In late 1977 I met Anthony Leicester, a former RAF pilot, over my patio fence in Fort Lauderdale, and we married in July 1979.

After Magda Liguori left Dakar in 1961 I corresponded with her until 1975, when her letters from Buenos Aires suddenly stopped. In 1999, twenty-four years later, my husband and I took a tri-continental cruise, from Buenos Aires to Barcelona, stopping at ports along the Brazilian coast, crossing to Madiera, then Dakar, Gibraltar and Morocco. The main purpose of this cruise was to find Magda, revisit Dakar, and show Tony around Morocco. He wanted me to see where he had landed in Gibraltar during the war.

As soon as we got to our hotel from the Buenos Aires airport we started searching for Magda. I suspected that she was one of the "Disappeared" (those opposed to the military regime of Argentina). She was the perfect type, an artist, writer, intellectal and rebel. She was not listed in the phone directory. No surprise. In the past twenty four years she could have married, or moved away. We did find the address of *Madres de Plaza de Mayo*, mothers of the disappeared, who march in protest every Thursday in the Plaza. It was miles away according to our city map. By this time jet lag claimed us and our efforts for the day ceased.

The following day we walked all the way to the Madre's address, a shoddy old office building in the blue-collar workers' district. Afraid they would not understand my poor Spanish, I reluctantly rang the bell. A young man opened the door and seemed surprised to see two elderly Americans. I told him that we were looking for the Madres. He said they no longer had an office. He must have noticed the disappointment on our faces and said that this was the headquarters of a similar organization and invited us in.

Luckily the young man in charge, Juan, spoke English. I showed him photos of Magda and articles about her paintings. He scrutinized her pixie face, framed by short black hair and lit by intelligent dark eyes. He said he didn't know her, but he photocopied the articles and photos to show to Las Madres. Then taking a dog-eared book (list of *Los Desaparacedos*) from the rickety shelf, below a space heater strapped to the wall, he placed it on a roughhewn wooden table, littered with papers. He searched all the variations of Magda's last name, but found nothing.

I handed him a nineteen-year-old yellowed newspaper clippings of Adofo Perez Esquivel, a sculptor, who received the Nobel Peace Prize in 1980 for standing up against the Military Junta. "Do you know him?" I asked.

"Yes," he said. "He has an office in this building, but he's not here today. We are getting ready for a big demonstration tomorrow in the Plaza de Mayo." He added that Perez was about Magda's age and might know her. Juan scribbled his phone number on a scrap of paper and asked me to call the day after the demonstration. We left with high hopes of finding Magda. My mind was full of pictures of our meeting. The young Magda would now be almost sixty, but in my memory she was always twenty-nine, the way she looked in the newspaper pictures I carried with me.

The next evening at six o'clock we went to the Plaza de Mayo to attend the demonstration and meet Perez (we hoped). As we waited for the organizers to set up the PA system, we sat on a crowded bench and watched the plaza fill with people. The Police methodically cordoned off the streets, Black Marias one by one pulled up to block intersections, and armed policemen slowly surrounded the square. Darkness hovered and thunder clouds threatened. The atmosphere was eerie. We got cold feet, left the bench to an eager couple with a baby and pushed our way through the crowd, crossed through the police line and walked back to the hotel.. arriving in the dark.

The next morning I called Juan and told him that we didn't stay for the demonstration. He said it was successful although we saw nothing in the newspaper. Perez knew of Magda, he said, but didn't know her personally. He hadn't seen her in years and knew nothing of her whereabouts.

But I was determined and we set out to find Magda's last address. Another few miles by foot. (We were really getting to know B.A.) Her last address turned out to be an updated apartment building with a locked wrought-iron gate and three buttons outside. I rang one. A woman answered and said she had never heard of Magda. The other buttons didn't answer. We went next door to the shoemaker. Luckily we understood one another's Spanish and had a lengthy talk, during which he kept studying Magda's pictures. He had been there forty years, but he didn't know Magda and didn't remember ever seeing her, or hearing her family name. He suggested I go to the radio station and give her name to the missing persons program, but alas we were leaving the following day.

Defeated, we left his shop and headed back when I saw a woman, 40ish, in jogging clothes, with a big German Shepherd on a leash, unlocking the door to the building where Magda used to live. I ran to her before she could get inside. Startled, but kind, she looked at the photos and clippings of Magda's art exhibits and then said that she was from Patagonia and had lived in the apartment only two years.

We didn't understand one another's Spanish, but she was determined to help and before we knew it we were on a tiny elevator to her apartment (which might have been Magda's mother's at one time). She sat us at the dining table near the phone, offered us a drink, lit a Malboro and dialed her husband's office. He spoke perfect English and suggested we call the landlord, which we did. He said the Liguori family left about twenty years ago and he didn't know their whereabouts. That didn't stop our "hostess" who called her father-in-law in Rio Negra because she thought there was a famous Liguori family living in that town. It wasn't the same family. By the time she called a few more people and even brought in the next door neighbor, we began feeling a bit weird and tried to leave. This nervous, chain-smoking woman wouldn't let us go. She begged us to stay for the midday meal, or come to dinner. We finally got out the door after much hugging and kissing and her promises to keep up the search and call us at our hotel. But I had lost hope. Sadly, we had come to a dead end. (I called her before we left, thanked her and told her the outcome.)

Trudging back to our hotel we passed an art gallery. The name seemed familiar. "Isn't that the gallery that sells the Persian-influenced paintings we saw last night at the waterfront restaurant," I asked Tony, taking out the card given me by the Maitre D'. It was. The young twenty-something man in charge (who understood my Spanish) invited us in, closed shop and took us to the second floor where we saw more of the artist's paintings. On the way back down the stairs, Tony whispered, "Ask him about Magda." I was reluctant, but Tony urged me. I showed him Magda's picture and asked if he knew her. When I said I hadn't heard from her since 1975. He smiled. "That was before I was born."

We thanked him for showing us his gallery, shook hands and started for the door.

"*Momento!*" he called out as he moved to the big desk in the corner, opened a drawer and took out a large book (Biographies of Argentinean Artists), turned to the L's, put his finger on Magda's name and handed the book to me. "Magda Liguori." I translated, "died in a tragic accident in 1975. She was forty years old." Through tears I could see a long list of her accomplishments, but I don't remember them. The search had ended. The mystery of her silence had been solved.

Ten days later we entered Dakar harbor. I was excited, expecting to feel some connection in spite of the warnings and horror stories about the Senegalese from the ship's briefing officer. I thought he was exaggerating. After all, I had lived there for almost two years. But when we descended the gangplank and felt the grabbing hands of insistent taxi drivers, in long Arab-like robes, speaking a crude version of French, we decided to take the ship's shuttle bus into town.

We got off at Independence Square. Although the American Embassy, where I had worked thirty seven years ago, was on the corner of the square, I felt as though I'd never been there. (Unlike when I returned to New Delhi, where I saw ghosts of myself everywhere.) The square seemed bigger, a new international hotel now claimed one side, but the Telegraph office, where I used to take encoded messages, to be sent out, was still there. I asked a man in the street to direct me to the American Embassy. It took several tries before we could understand one another's French. I never really understood his directions, but he pointed toward the Cathedral some distance away. I suspected a new embassy had been built, but I wanted to find the old one and he knew nothing about it. After examining the only possible building on the square I saw a clue: a rusted flag pole where the Stars and stripes used to fly. I looked up at the balcony, where I had burned secret trash in the dark of night, but I still couldn't connect. Thirty seven years had been a long time.

Following directions toward the cathedral we went in search of the new American Embassy, hoping to locate a friend, UN employee posted to Dakar. Careful of our footing we made our way through the heat and dust, over sidewalks broken by tree roots, or holes where pavement used to be, toward the only landmark I recognized, the Presidential Palace. The Guards made us cross to the other side of the street, but were kind to point in the direction to the U.S. Embassy.

Behind barricades and well guarded, the Embassy was a new, ordinary fortress-like building. We entered through the guard's gate, about the size of a closet, showed our passports, signed in, gave up our camera and went through a metal detector into a courtyard, then through the main entrance.

The young African male receptionist didn't understand either my French or my English when I said I was looking for a friend, Quinby, who worked at the UN Migration Organization. Getting no response, I moved a few feet to the bulletproof glass window and spoke through a slot to a Marine guard. He looked in a book and said there were no Q's listed. He didn't seem to know about the UN organization and was obviously not interested in further conversation even though I offered my friend's phone number.

Frustrated and put off I was about to leave when an embassy officer appeared. I told him that I was a retired Foreign Service Officer and was once posted to Dakar. He wasn't impressed. Begrudgingly he hesitated long enough to look in the official phone directory and make a call. He found out that my friend's organization had moved out of the city. He gave me the address and then turned to leave. I asked where I could find a phone to call my friend, hoping he would let me use the Embassy phone as we had no local money. "There's a phone at the cafe across the street," he said and left me standing there with not a single local coin and the African guard didn't know where we could change dollars.

Now I see why Americans abroad complain about our Embassy's treatment when they need help. I understand why our Embassy in Paris, or London, wouldn't have time to help every

Tom, Dick and Harry, but in Senegal (a really dangerous place) how many Americans come asking for help?

We decided to call later from the ship. Meanwhile, we went looking for the house where I used to live. We got lost. As we milled about trying to get our bearings I saw a corner gate in a wall, topped by hedge. It was Number 8, my old number, but I didn't recognize the surroundings and was about to leave when a lovely young woman approached. "What is the name of this street?" I asked. "Avenue Roosevelt," she replied, obviously understanding my French. My old street! My old house! Through a peephole I saw the garden where my servant, Mamadou, used to spread his prayer rug three times a day and pray to Allah. The latticework front porch had been closed in. The house, painted green when I lived there, was now flamingo pink. Again I felt no connection and saw no ghosts of myself. Maybe, unlike India, I had no affinity to Senegal and was never really "at home" in Dakar.

Before returning to the ship we had one more stop; the apartment where my Senegalese friend, Amy Sow, and her family had lived. On the way we found ourselves in front of the Canadian Embassy, housed on the fourth floor of a big office building. "Maybe they can help us," Tony suggested. We went up the steps, entered the door, got on the elevator, went up two floors and there we were. No guards anywhere! (No need to barricade themselves from enemies.) The handsome Senegalese receptionist greeted us in beautiful English and wanted to know how he could help us. Tony introduced himself as a Canadian citizen, showed his passport and told him we were looking for an American friend and gave him all the details. He immediately got on the phone, located the UN office. No answer. He commented that the UN people were not very conscientious.

We stayed there for half an hour and he called every few minutes between visitors. No reply. Before we left he said he would keep trying and asked where we were staying. Alas, we told him, we would be leaving in a few hours. Buoyed by his kindness (such a contrast to the treatment we'd got at the American Embassy) we set out to find Amy, the university student who had helped me learn French and connected me to her country and way of life.

After a long walk, through narrow, dirty, crowded back streets, we found the apartment building where she used to live with her family. It was in bad repair, as was most of Dakar. We arrived just as some young people emerged from the building. I ask about the Sow family. They had never heard of them. "How long ago?" asked a pretty young woman in a flowing robe, "did they live here?" When I said Thirty-seven years her friends burst into laughter and said, "They're probably dead by now." To these young people thirty-seven years was a lifetime.

Later, as the ship left the harbor, I leaned on the rail, watched Dakar sink into the darkness and thought of Charles—Louis, Bounette and all my French friends and wondered where they were.

At dinner that night my table mates asked how could I have been happy in such a terrible, poverty-ridden place. I assured them that it wasn't like that when I lived there. French influence was still strong for one thing and for another I made lots of friends, French, English and Senegalese. It was not my favorite post, I admitted, but I managed to find the bright side. "Besides," I said, "happiness comes from inside."

END